I0140080

THE DAUGHTERS OF THE MOON

Part One
of
The City of the Bayou
Collection

Reginald Edmund

BROADWAY PLAY PUBLISHING INC
New York
www.broadwayplaypublishing.com
info@broadwayplaypublishing.com

THE DAUGHTERS OF THE MOON
© Copyright 2021 Reginald Edmund

All rights reserved. This work is fully protected under the copyright laws of the United States of America. No part of this publication may be photocopied, reproduced, stored in a retrieval system, or transmitted, in any form or by any means, electronic, mechanical, recording, or otherwise, without the prior permission of the publisher. Additional copies of this play are available from the publisher.

Written permission is required for live performance of any sort. This includes readings, cuttings, scenes, and excerpts. For amateur and stock performances, please contact Broadway Play Publishing Inc. For all other rights please contact the author http://www.reginaldedmund.com.

Cover photo by Errol Wilks

First edition: June 2021
I S B N: 978-0-88145-863-3

Book design: Marie Donovan
Page make-up: Adobe InDesign
Typeface: Palatino

Dedicated to
my grandmothers
Isabel Green and Edwynne Harrison,
my wife Simeilia Hodge-Dallaway,
my mother Geneva Winfield,
my mentor Marie Marcel,
and to all Black Women as they go on their journey.

Special Dedication to Detria Ward (1962-2019)

The City of the Bayou Collection is a series of nine plays. They are the playwright's attempt at making a contemporary House of Atreus through a Afro-Surrealist lens. The plays, in order, are:

THE DAUGHTERS OF THE MOON

SOUTHBRIDGE

IN THE PROPHET'S HOUSE

BLOOD ON THE BAYOU

REDEMPTION OF ALLAH BLACK

JUNETEENTH STREET

THE ORDAINED SMILE OF SAINT SADIE MAY JENKINS

THE LAST CADILLAC

ALL THE DYING VOICES

THE DAUGHTERS OF THE MOON received its first workshop reading at Chicago Dramatists Theatre.

This workshop was followed by a staged readings 3-4 April 2015 by The Department of Dramatic Arts and Department of Music at University of Connecticut—Storrs Campus.

THE DAUGHTERS OF THE MOON premiered on 17 May 2017 in Houston TX, produced by the University Players Alumni Association (Texas Southern University) in collaboration with the De LUXE Theater in Historical Fifth Ward. The cast and creative contributors were:

MAWU...Detria Ward
KOKUMA/ABIGAIL ....Susan Loren
JULIA ELIZABETH.....................................An'Gelle Sylvester
SPIRIT NORTH, LIBRANCE BROTHERS ....Alicia Stevens
SPIRIT SOUTH, SLAVE AUCTIONEER,
    PEARSON...Jessica Johnson
SPIRIT EAST, SCRATCH.. Crystal Rae
SPIRIT WEST, KOKUMA'S MOTHER .... Daisha Nash

Director..Timothy Eric
Production manager ....Errol Anthony Wilks
Stage manager...................... Arianna Day & Lauren Julun
Scenic, lighting & sound design ....Timothy Eric
Costume design .... Toni Whitaker
Hair & make-up design........................... Roenia Thompson
Properties design..Timothy Eric
                                          & Rachel Hemphill Dickson
Fight choreographer ....Kelvin Hamilton
Scenic / wardrobe assistant.............................Molly Hurley
House management........T S U University Players Alumni
                                                                    Association

CHARACTERS & SETTING

MAWU, *Goddess of the Moon, Beautiful, Timeless*

KOKUMO / ABIGAIL, *thirteen years old, her name means "immortal", she's blessed.*

JULIA ELIZABETH, MR LIBRANCE'S *wife, wealthy*

CHORUS (NORTH, SOUTH, EAST, *and* WEST), *the winds they take upon them the role of characters they meet in this strange land called America.*

Place: An Empty Theatre, Africa, The Raging Ocean, the Slave block, the Cruelities of America

NOTE

No preshow music only the sound of a drum or of a racing beating heart, chorus roles although written out aren't completely locked to those characters.

BOOK ONE
THE GODDESS SPEAKS

(An empty space. Dim light. Suddenly, a lone woman, MAWU, *enters the room carrying a large ornate walking stick. She's shabbily wearing an old coat, and a large beaten-up church going hat. There's something ancient about her, timeless but beautiful.)*

(She walks toward us surveys the room and speaks.)

MAWU: Awon omo mi … Awon omo mi … Mi lẹwa obinrin ati awon omo mi bi daradara. Gbo mi bayi. Jẹ mi so fun o kan itan…

(Translation Yoruba: My children… My children… My beautiful daughters and my sons as well. Hear me now. Let me tell you a story…)

(She pauses as she realizes that no one in the audience understands her.)

Ah Ah… *(She'll try another.)* My ụmụ… My ụmụ…

(Translation Igbo: My children… My children…)

(Again she pauses as she realizes that no one in the audience understands her. Finally she catches on…)

Ah I see you've forgotten the tongue of your people… sad. For what is a people if they do not know their stories. Their songs. Me… You've forgotten me. The one who watched over you at night. My name is… I've had many… More names than I can remember… You've called me so many…Gleti, Bendis, Thoth, Iah, Khonsu, Kalfu, Yemaya… But call me Mawu. Goddess of the moon. Illuminator of truth. Let me tell you a story my children, listen to me now my sons and daughters to this story written in the stars long ago. This story of sorrow and of love. That is the story I shall tell you about two broken souls... one a girl stolen from her ancient home and a woman brokened hearted both battered by this cruel land you now call home...America. This is their story. And their story is ours. Perhaps the spirits shall help me tell this story.

(MAWU *pounds the walking stick to the earth. The sound of African drums fill the room. She beats the walking stick to the earth once...twice...three times. The old garb come off of her and she stands there in an elegant African garb. She's a priestess. No a queen... No she's more than that she's a Goddess. She raises her arms upward and begins to speak.*)

(MAWU *speaks as she calls forth the* WINDS...NORTH, SOUTH, EAST, *and* WEST *enter the stage singing.*)

CHORUS: (*Sings as they enter overlapping* MAWU's *words*)
Ose ayo,
A-beh A-deh o,
Ah-eh-o
(*X 5*)

(*Each wind as they sing creates the world around her. The sun overhead, the river, and the mountains, and the valley lo. The continent of Africa, that ancient place called Kemet is shaped from their hands.*)

MAWU: Picture a place born from my flesh, kissed by my moonlight kisses. Kissed so many times that's become me. Every part of me mirrored in this most holy of places. I stretch out my arms to the world, I am this land once known as Kemet. My hair the Okavango Delta, the Omo, and the Nile, my fingers and toes stretch out far and wide to create Mt. Kilimanjaro, Mosi-oa-Tunya, Ngorongoro, Maasai Mara, the Serengeti, the curve of my breasts the Mulanje Massif, my feet the Forests of the Baobabs, and right here, between my breasts, where my heart is… where I hold all that is most sacred to me I want you to imagine a village, oh it's a beautiful village. It rests right along the coast line, siting upon a beach.

SOUTH: Beautifully white sand, water crisp clear… so clear you can see your way to the bottom of the ocean floor.

WEST: Lining the village the pungent sweet smell of the agbayun and the white and scarlet flowers called the bleeding glory fills the air mixes with the sound of children laughing, playing…

EAST: The men fishing and food plentiful, and the women singing as the care for the young. Raising their strong fine-looking children… Crackling fires, the air a ceaseless warm breeze…

NORTH: The sky above its… Gold. Red. Blue. Endless endless spectrums of blue. Here in this place if you are quiet and still long enough you can feel the gods smiling down upon this place.

MAWU: This place is like…

CHORUS: Heaven.

MAWU: Or the closest you'll get to it walking this earth. In this place, our storytellers are born. Here the first woman shaped by the clay and kissed by my lips was formed. From her all life was created. This holy place… The gods, my brothers and sisters in the sky all recognized it as such, divine. This place is what's the word… Sacred…for it's the way this world should have been all along. A place of love. Now in this village, this favorite of my villages there lives a girl. Her name is…

(MAWU *conjures her* [KOKUMA] *from out of what seems like thin air.*)

CHORUS: Kokuma.

KOKUMA: They call me Kokuma.

MAWU: Oh and she is blessed.

SOUTH: A beautiful beautiful kissed by the earth, grey eyed child.

MAWU: She was a grey-eyed brown skinned child.

EAST: Mischief and curiosity in her heart.

NORTH: Born of a long generation of seers.

MAWU: In the day when she wasn't learning the ways of the griots, and the priestesses, she'd help her mother do the errands and tend to the house and at night as the sound of the ocean waves crash against the beach of the tiny peaceful village her mother would sing to her as she combed Kokuma's hair.

KOKUMA: Owwww… Yeye so hard

WEST: (As MOTHER) Sit still little girl.
How did I ever get a child with such a hard behind, and such a tender head?

KOKUMA: I'm not tender headed you just comb my hair so rough, Yeye. You keep that up I'll have no hair left to comb.

WEST: (As MOTHER) You are such a silly girl, now quit fidgeting I'm almost done.

KOKUMA: Ow, Yeye

WEST: (As MOTHER) Sometimes to obtain beauty you need to experience a little pain.

KOKUMA: Well I think I can live without pain then mama.

WEST: (As MOTHER) You wait and see, child, you'll miss the days of your mama brushing and combing your hair. Cherish these moments now.

KOKUMA: Ow, Yeye!!!

WEST: (*As* MOTHER) There… all done.

KOKUMA: Can I go outside and play now?

WEST: (*As* MOTHER) It's so late

KOKUMA: Please Yeye, just for a little while before bed.

WEST: (*As* MOTHER) You can my child. But remember no matter what, do not play near the holy fire.

KOKUMA: Yes, Yeye.

WEST: (*As* MOTHER) Why do I say don't play by the holy fire?

KOKUMA: Cause it allows the Mother Moon to look over us and protect us all.

WEST: (*As* MOTHER) Yes that is right my child. Now be off then. Be good.

KOKUMA: I will, Yeye.

East and South turn into children, North a villager.

MAWU: Off she went, that beautiful mischievous child I love… Off to play with Afia and Oni. They danced around the village and ran along the beach. Their feet kicking up sand and their laughter filled the air.
(*To audience*)
Beach turned to grass as they dodged tree branches and weaved through trees that soon turned to forest that hide the sacred village and they found themselves standing in front of the holy fire.

KOKUMA: Stop

EAST: What? Why?

KOKUMA: We can't go near the holy fire.

EAST: Says who?

KOKUMA: Say my Yeye, says the whole village.

SOUTH: Kokuma, you can't possibly believe that this one stupid little fire keeps this whole village hidden from the world.

KOKUMA: I do.

EAST: Why cause your Yeye, the priestess says so?

KOKUMA: Yes

EAST: What does that old woman know?

KOKUMA: Don't talk about my Yeye. She's the wisest woman in the village.

EAST: Then prove it. Prove that's she's right.

KOKUMA: How?

(EAST and SOUTH look at each other and then look to KOKUMA.)

EAST & SOUTH: Blow out the fire.

KOKUMA: I can't do that.

SOUTH: What's the matter you scared?

KOKUMA: I fear nothing.

SOUTH: Then do it. Watch nothing will happen.

KOKUMA: Fine then I'll do it.
(She moves to the flame.)

EAST: Will she do it?

SOUTH: She won't do it.

EAST: She'll do it…

SOUTH: She won't… I'm telling you she won't…

(KOKUMA moves to the flame.)

KOKUMA: Quit telling me what I will and will not do. Slowly I approach the fire and I blow and…
(She blows out the fire and…nothing happens.)

EAST: See told ya so.

What does your yeye know, but stories passed on from one fool to the other to keep children's eyes closed at night.

KOKUMA: No blacken sky, no thunder and lightning, rain, or howling winds raging out… just silence. Just strange lonely silence.
Separate from the world. Mawu appears from the darkness. A singular piece of her garment falls to the earth.

MAWU: Oh my child, what have you done?

KOKUMA: What could this mean? Did my Yeye lie to me?
Do the gods truly watch over us? Do they even exist? We swore to tell no one and rushed to our separate homes. I tossed and turned in my sleep.

(As KOKUMA sleeps, the WINDS huddle around her and dance.)

EAST & NORTH: That night they fall asleep but wake up to the sound of thunder.

EAST: And thunder.

NORTH: And thunder.

CHORUS: Followed by the cries of fear and death.

(End scene)

BOOK TWO
THE ENDLESS SEA

(MAWU shines brightly standing high overhead as KOKUMA steps out of the darkness and she never looks upward towards the moon.)

KOKUMA: I don't know if you'll hear me. I pray that you'll feel something in your souls… Maybe you will…

Maybe you won't. I tell this tale and if the goddess of
the moon hears my prayers you'll listen. You'll feel
something. I've learned overtime that just like my
people pray to the moon and the stars above, that the
white mans' god is death. I will never forget that night.
Try as hard as I can pull up that memory like a weed
and rip it away, it still haunts me. Never leaves. Never
goes… That night we fall asleep to the sound of joy,
of love, of mothers tucking in their children, of men
laughing with their brothers, of cattle braying, the
drums beating, and the ocean crashing against the
sandy shores. That night we fall asleep but wake up
to the sound of thunder. And thunder. And thunder.
Followed by the cries of fear and death. I sat up. Fear
beating in my heart.

CHORUS: Shadows outside running. Screams.

KOKUMA: I open my mouth to scream as well, but my
mother stops me.

MAWU: We must run, my child.

KOKUMA: She says. She drags me by the hand. Pulls
hard…never seen fear upon her face like that before.
"Where's father" I say. She looks at me. "Where's
father!!!" I say but that look on her face is enough of an
answer for me.

SOUTH: She answer eerily calm.

WEST: Tears and fear held back.

MAWU: With the ancestors now.

KOKUMA: Run…

CHORUS: Thunder…

KOKUMA: Run…

CHORUS: Thunder…

KOKUMA: When I fall she would pull me up. We ran
weaving through the trees, stumbling, falling, picking

ourselves back up again hiding whenever we could. Don't look back. All I hear is the sound of fire burning huts, the sound of screams, the sound of the thunder and more thunder. The sound of the oceans waves crashing again the shore. And death.

EAST: SHHHHH

KOKUMA: And death.

WEST: SHHHHHH

KOKUMA: And Death.

MAWU: Ssssshhhhh… Listen to me child, listen to me, We must run and never look back, our home is gone from us. We must go my child. Stay low. Stay quiet. No matter what you see you can not scream.

KOKUMA: Before she could take me away from here. A man grabbed her.

SOUTH: A pale skin man,

NORTH: Wild beard,

EAST: Eyes hateful.

NORTH: He carried death in one hand.

EAST: She didn't let out a scream.

SOUTH: As the blood bubbled from her mouth,

KOKUMA: I was an obedient child…
I made no sound.
All I could do is watch as she dropped to her knees and embraced the soil. The man wiped my mother's precious blood from his face and motioned for the men to take me away. And then I fell into a dreamless sleep, I wish it had been death.

(MAWU *sings mournfully in Yoruba and cradles* KOKUMA *in her arms. The moonlight shines down upon them.*)

MAWU:
Ose ayo,
A-beh A-deh o,
Ah-eh-o
(X 3)

KOKUMA: Mother Moon.

MAWU *(To* KOKUMA*)* Sleep child, sleep.
You are the last of my blessed ones.
You will have a long cruel journey ahead of you.
Across the angry seas and even harsher lands.
And many tests placed before you can touch freedom.
But know this.
I will be watching over you. Even when in times my
reach can not.

(Fades into darkness)

MAWU:
Ose ayo,
A-beh A-deh o,
Ah-eh-o
(X3)

(Slowly more voices join MAWU *as she sings. And more. Till the voices fills the darkness of the slave ship.)*

(The sound of the ocean, NORTH *and* SOUTH *create the noise of sailors calling out above deck, and then crying of chained thousands below. The chorus cries out. Echoes some of her words)*

NORTH: Hoist sails and be quick about it you bastards!!!

EAST & WEST: Hoist sails

NORTH: America bound!!!

(The sound of chains, as WEST *and* EAST *moan in agony.* NORTH *and* SOUTH *sing a sailors' song.)*

KOKUMA: I wake up in darkness the sound of the ocean still calling. Stripped down naked.

SOUTH: Surrounded by crying silhouettes.

WEST: The ones screaming turned to cries,

EAST: Cries turned to whimpers.

KOKUMA: Chained to rough wood. Chains bit into my skin. Chains Hot. Wrists bleeding. Parched. I wanted to vomit from the rough rocking of the ocean pounding angrily again the boat. Calling for them to free it's children.

CHORUS: Why?

KOKUMA: Why did you take my mother and my father from me?

CHORUS: Why?

KOKUMA: Why did you take me away from my home.

CHORUS: Why?!!!

KOKUMA: Why did you named me blessed one if I was to be cursed to this life? If I was to be cursed to see these horrors.
Why? Why? Why?!!!
I called out. But my goddess didn't answer.

NORTH: None of the gods answers…

WEST: No ancestor reached out to unshackle us from our bonds.

KOKUMA: All I heard was the crying of those around me in the darkness,

EAST: The jangling of chains being pulled against, and the waves of ocean pounding against the wood of the boat.

KOKUMA: The heat from the unseen sun and the bodies…

SOUTH: Pressed,

NORTH: Huddled,

WEST: Crammed against each other.

KOKUMA: Narrow shelves upon narrow shelves of bodies. My hands wrapping around the chains pulling with all my soul against the wood beam holding it fast, pulling until my muscles strained, my fingers bled…

WEST: Blisters…

EAST: Exhaustion…

SOUTH: Chains slippery with blood…

NORTH: Skin ripped from skin…

CHORUS: Here was sorrow…

KOKUMA: Here my living tomb.
Mother Moon, I cried why have you and the gods forsaken us?

CHORUS: Mother Moon…

KOKUMA: Hear my prayer… speak to me like you would in my village.
Tell me I will survive. Tell me you will watch after me.
Tell me I'm still blessed.
But I heard nothing.

WEST: Streams of sunlight streamed in and cut through the darkness.

EAST: But did nothing to distract from this horror.

KOKUMA: I closed my eyes. Took a deep breath of the stale air and listened quietly.

MAWU: My darling child, I'm looking for you. Where are you my child?

KOKUMA: But all I heard is the ocean,

SOUTH: The clanging of chains, the moans of the dying and the scared.

NORTH: Day became night,

EAST: Night became day,

WEST: And back again.

CHORUS: Over and over again.

KOKUMA: No moon…no silverish gleam of the Mother Moon reaching through the ceiling of our tomb to touch our faces and comfort us. Just cold darkness followed by streams of hot sunlight.

NORTH: Scraps of food.

SOUTH: Darkness and streams of sunlight.

NORTH: Scraps.

WEST: Darkness and sunlight.

NORTH: Scraps.

KOKUMA: Finally our caged tombs open. They pull us above and all we see is the blue of the sea, endless endless blue. No clue of where north, or south laid. And the face of my mothers killer on each of their faces. Some bearded, some not. Some blue eyed, some brown, some young, some old but they all held the faces of my mother's killer. They speak to each other in a tongue unknown to me.
In the daytime they make us dance. Douse us with the cold salty water of the sea.
At night…at night… They take some of the women and girls and on occasion a man too and find pleasure sweating hutched over their prizes laughing at their expense. I look around at my people.
The look of joy in their eyes they once had disappeared. Gone…I recognize a few faces from my village. There were Adena, Amara, Dzata,

SOUTH: The twins Kafui and Mawusi,

WEST: The fat nose one name Abrah, Anani, and Mensah,

NORTH: And more…

CHORUS: And more…

(As KOKUMA speaks the CHORUS speaks in round.)

CHORUS: Darkness and streams of sunlight.
Scraps.
Darkness and sunlight.
Scraps.
Darkness…

KOKUMA: It was comforting knowing I wasn't alone. A mother kisses her child, holds her close, she looks towards one, and they look towards another and another… A Nod amongst them all and she jumps child in her arms to their death. She carried those chained with her over as well. They couldn't find freedom in this life they'll find it in the next.
I sighed a quiet prayer for them and wish I was as brave as her to meet death that way.
Angry shouts from the pale skin men.
Somehow I knew the deaths would prove to be costly for them.
Tossed back into our cages below deck…
Just cold darkness followed by streams of hot sunlight.
Scraps of food.
The ocean…pitched and roared…

(KOKUMA and MAWU cram close to each other, shackles wrapped around Mawu's walking stick… as the ship pitched angrily upon the sea, they too are tossed about. It's an heart wrenching funeral dance that remains moving in every direction but anchored to the floor they sit… Their bodies huddled and broken their eyes looking upward.)

KOKUMA: The ocean rolled and roared…

CHORUS: Rolled and roared.

KOKUMA: The ocean rocked and roared…

CHORUS: Rocked and roared…

KOKUMA: As I lay in the darkness I see light. Silver-ish light of mother moon stretch her fingers out and reach for me through the ceiling of our cage. I strain for my face to touch the light.

MAWU: My child, I have found you.
I have found you my child, and I will not let you go.

CHORUS: We beg you… Free us Mother Moon.

MAWU: I can't my children.

KOKUMA: Free us Mother Moon.

MAWU: I can't.

KOKUMA: Then leave me, there are children here. Children younger than me. Free them. Let them go. Let them never know this sorrow. Free them. Take them away.

MAWU: Oh my brave girl… I can't my child. The light of the moon can't touch the chains that hold you hostage…

KOKUMA: So all is lost?

MAWU: No my child. Let me leave you a gift.

KOKUMA: A gift?

MAWU: Come closer, can you reach the light?

KOKUMA: I think so.

MAWU: Try… Come closer.

KOKUMA: I strain my face forward more, pulling at the chain and the moon light touches my face. In a world of perfect darkness it cuts through the pitch blackness and kisses me.

Caresses me with her light. Fills me with a warmth I've never known before… A flame ignites deep in my heart. She was me and I was her. I could feel her all around me. She was with me, but not. I was there but floating above myself. Looking down upon this fragile chained grey eyed girl. Tiny, slender, Not beautiful but pretty.

I wanted to leave that scared little girl's body behind… Her face craned upward eyes closed, chains cutting deeply into her wrists, blood slowly dripping from her cuts puddling on that rough wood floor and then I felt myself pulled back into myself. I open my eyes and the stream of moonlight is gone. Just me and the hundreds upon hundreds of bodies trapped upon the wooden cage floating upon the endless-endless ocean. I knew I wasn't alone on this journey. Mother Moon was with me and I knew with her hand guiding me that soon… Soon… No matter what it took I was going to find my way to freedom.

(KOKUMA *looks up raises her shackled hand high and pulls the shackles breaking them as the stage becomes covered in darkness.*)

(*End scene*)

BOOK THREE
COLD GREY WORLD

(*America… The sound of the streets outside during the 1800s. Carriages over cobblestone. The chirping of birds, the commotion one hears in a city of industry…*)

(*The sound of a ships docking at port.* JULIA ELIZABETH *appears, she appears lost. She notices the audience and smiles.*)

JULIA ELIZABETH: Once a month my dear husband makes a trip down to New Orleans from our home

outside of Biloxi, to purchase new property for the
plantation but truth tell it's just another opportunity
to lay around with his whores. This day was different
though seeing as how it was our anniversary, he
decided to bring me along so I can pick myself a new
girl to wait on me. Seeing as how last one he bought
for me, he happened to catch a fancy to. And a girl he
catch fancy to finds themselves falling off balconies. He
told me he'd make amend for his bastard ways. Find
me a young one. One too young for his carnal desires
or so he says. City life in the south is not quite to my
liking. Makes me miss Boston. Folks seem to flock
to New Orleans like pilgrims. Dressed in their finest
attire it does them absolutely no good in my opinion,
masking the filth of the place as the city spews down
upon the poor souls soft grey ash belched down from
the hundreds of factory chimneys that reach out high
above. New Orleans as colorful as that place is, to me
it's a dull uncivilized world. Not like my home with
father in Boston. Pulling me hard through the filthy
streets. My husband was always a driven minded
man that one. We weave through the dirtiness of the
city, Mr Librance pushing through the crowded city
streets ahead of me. Leading me to a dirty port filled
with warehouses. He pulled me towards one of them
and knocks upon a great wooden door. Once…twice…
three times. Librance loved to break laws whenever he
could and he liked his stock exotic. Here they held the
illegal auction. Hundreds of half-naked men, women,
children lined up. Scrawny. Dirty.

(The NORTH WIND *speaks as if channeling* MR LIBRANCE.)

NORTH: Julia darling, I know they don't look much
currently but remember now when you're in the
market for a young negress, to disregard their present
condition, think about three things, dear, do they look
like they carry the disposition to be properly broken for

house servitude, whether they possess the possibility for future resell, and lastly do they look like when they get too old for the house whether they'd breed proper stock farther on down the line…

(The SOUTH WIND *turns into the auctioneer.)*

SOUTH: Here we go ladies and gentlemen, hear we go…
We got ourselves some right fine ones to be purchased right here.

JULIA ELIZABETH: Tall ones

SOUTH: Ladies and gents, can I get two hundred dollars as an opening bid?

EAST: Two hundred dollars

JULIA ELIZABETH: Short ones

SOUTH: Do we got two hundred fifty?

WEST: Two hunred fifty.

JULIA ELIZABETH: Old ones.

SOUTH: Can I get three hunred?

EAST: Three hundred.

JULIA ELIZABETH: Young ones

SOUTH: Can I get three hundred fifty, ladies and gents? This one is prime for breeding young niglets.

JULIA ELIZABETH: Women stripped naked clutching children tightly in their arms. Bellies swelling with life, breasts full…

SOUTH: Four hunderd, these two come in a pair or we can give them to you separately

EAST & WEST: Four hundred.

JULIA ELIZABETH: Watched as mothers screamed and cried as their children pulled from them.

SOUTH: Five hundred for the young midnight black bull. Do I hear five hundred.

JULIA ELIZABETH: Broad shouldered men, backs already raw and scarring from the whips.

EAST: Five hundred fifty.

SOUTH: YES!!! We got five hundred fifty you good Christian ladies and gents.

JULIA ELIZABETH: There eyes all had the same look to them, they carried with it the look of ones defeated…

SOUTH: Six hundred.

JULIA ELIZABETH: Dejected…

SOUTH: Seven hundred.

JULIA ELIZABETH: Broken.

SOUTH: Seven hundred fifty, can I get a seven fifty.

CHORUS: Seven hundred and fifty dollars.

JULIA ELIZABETH: And then out of the multitude upon multitude of dark skin that paraded by there stood a small girl. At first glance there wasn't anything that truly remarkable about her in appearance, a runt of a girl, twelve maybe thirteen at the oldest but there she was. There she was. I was drawn to her. Pulled to her. Pushed through the crowd to get a closer look at her. She was just a girl, scrawny malnourished but those eyes.

CHORUS: Those silver grey eyes

JULIA ELIZABETH: They carved through the people before her. I approached her looked her over and her eyes never strayed from me. Blood dripped from her chained wrists, she flinched at first as I reached towards her but stood her ground unwavered, no fear in her eyes. Defiance maybe? Eyes that seemed to hold

the secrets of the cold world within them. What did this tiny girl know that the rest of the world didn't? I grasp her wrists and examine them.
It looked like the shackles had bit into flesh where the soft curve of her wrists are...what looked like crescent moons.

MAWU: Eyes meet eyes.

(MAWU *takes their hands connects them.*)

(MAWU *bangs her staff.*)

(*The world parts open.*)

JULIA ELIZABETH: The girl, this little girl reaches out touches the ivory broach shaped like the crescent moon pinned to my blouse. The one my great grandmother had brought from the old country long ago, the one that she passed down to her daughter, her daughter passed on to me. I wanted to back way but something held me fast. Held me in place.

(NORTH *speaks to her as if she's* JULIA ELIZABETH's *husband.*)

NORTH: (LIBRANCE) Julia...Julia, dear it's bad form to be touching the merchandise unless you're going to buy them. They don't take kindly to that.

JULIA ELIZABETH / MAWU: This one.

NORTH: What?

JULIA ELIZABETH: This one.

NORTH: She's a runt of a girl, dear, barely be able to carry your trays during evening tea for you.

JULIA ELIZABETH: I want this one. This girl.

NORTH: Julia Elizabeth.
She's not a worthy investment, look at the girl.

JULIA ELIZABETH: You said did you not that I can get any young negress I want?

NORTH: I did.

JULIA ELIZABETH: Then this is her.

SOUTH: Seven hundred fifty can I get a seven hundred fifty.

JULIA ELIZABETH: A fierce bidding war took place between my husband and another gentlemen.

SOUTH: Eight hundred.
Eight hundred twenty-five.
Eight hundred fifty, can I get eight hundred fifty, eight hundred fifty to the man in the red hat.
Eight hundred seventy-five.
Nine hundred?
Do I have nine hundred dollars?

CHORUS: Sold.

SOUTH: Highest amount ever bidded for a child negress.

CHORUS: Congrats to the winner.

JULIA ELIZABETH: She was mine. I would name her Abigail…Mr Librance didn't approve. I named her after the daughter I had lost still born long ago. It wasn't that long afterwards we had gathered up our purchase. Placed her in the back of the carriage and made our way back home again. I loved Mr Librance that day. Only time I ever could remember loving him.

WEST: Hard to love a man that cruel.

EAST: A man that would ravage his wife on their wedding day, force his desires upon her.

WEST: A man that took to his drink and to his whores.

EAST: A man that rage upon and beat his wife like he would his slaves.

SOUTH: Was there any difference?

JULIA ELIZABETH: I'd think to myself some nights as I laid bruised and battered, other than the fact my skin was white. Hair slicked back, constantly looking to his gold watch attached to his vest. He was a cruel man, but on that day. As that little grey eyed colored girl rode behind us on that carriage ride back home I loved him.

CHORUS: Strange this world we live in.

JULIA ELIZABETH: Stranger still our emotions.

MAWU: Oh, how a single action can change our feelings and attractions.

(Lights shift. Days and months pass.)

MAWU: Blues become green, green become yellows, yellows become blue.

JULIA ELIZABETH: Abigail took to her duties well. Either myself or one of my servants would show her the duties, she'd have to take on and she'd take to them. Right quick…

CHORUS: Smart she was.

JULIA ELIZABETH: She never spoke, quiet, not a word… Mr. Librance considered her dumb and a fools investment, called her…

NORTH: She's just a damn play thing and little negra doll to you isn't she, Julia.

JULIA ELIZABETH: Claimed…

NORTH: You know dear, We could have gotten three negras the amount we wasted on that girl.

JULIA ELIZABETH: But I could always tell that she unnerved the man a bit. Of course it didn't ease matter in the least bit that the help around the house whispered…

CHORUS: That girl's a witch.

JULIA ELIZABETH: I saw no sign of it. Save for those grey eyes. Always looking at me with those grey eyes. Some days she'd sit by the balcony and a large crow would land resting on the balcony beside her. In the quiet evenings before bed she'd brush my hair. A hundred strokes to my hair with my brush before trimming the ends with a pair of scissors from my dresser. She'd hum as she brushed my hair every night. She was an obedient child. And before I wandered off to sleep I'd read to her when I could for I had no child of my own to read to. Did she understand the words I said to her? That I don't know. But she'd sit there. Always listening. A year and a month that girl served with no problems. No word ever uttered from her lips… But on the thirteenth day of that thirteenth month, Mr Librance returned home one stormy night raging from the drink.

(The sound of drums beating like a racing heart beat and then thunder fills the air. The NORTH *appears as* LIBRANCE.*)*

JULIA ELIZABETH: I know what happens when the drink is in that man's spirit.
If it's not me getting beaten, then it's the girls being thrown out the window, or the girl he branded his name upon her thigh for all to know he mounted, or the one he buried up to the neck in the field leaving her for three days til she died thirsting for food and water, the need of food replaced by the gaping lifeless mouth full of flies, another he stomped upon her pregnant belly till the red fleshy jelly that was her child spewed from her womb.

CHORUS: Atrocities upon atrocities

JULIA ELIZABETH: Far more than I had fingers and toes to count.

All the tear stained brown skinned faces wasted ashen by death, stretched and hollowed peering at me in my mind.

NORTH: Gurl…come here.

CHORUS: Haunted me.

JULIA ELIZABETH: All those souls calling out to me…

MAWU: Don't let her follow the others fate.

NORTH: Gurl…come here.

JULIA ELIZABETH: How many times did I turn my eyes to the horrors he's committed.

MAWU: Save the child please.

JULIA ELIZABETH: How many times did I turn away, allow their suffering to save myself.

NORTH: Gurl…you see me talkin' to ya. Come here.

MAWU: Save her please.
He laughed and he laughed as he ran his fingers through his hair.

JULIA ELIZABETH: Whiskey reeked from his pores. Face red.

MAWU: Save her.

JULIA ELIZABETH: The sound of thunder came and went.
He stumbled drunkenly towards her.

JULIA ELIZABETH & NORTH: Such a pretty gurl, you are.

NORTH: Such a pretty gurl you are, bout time I get my money's worth… Come here gurl.

JULIA ELIZABETH: Over and over he'd say those words.

NORTH: Come here.
Come here.
You come here!

MAWU: SAVE HER.

JULIA ELIZABETH: RUN, CHILD!!!

MAWU: And run she did.

WEST: No servant in that house, in that field…woman or man would stand against the storm of rage that man possessed for fear of death.

JULIA ELIZABETH: Furniture tossed, my body thrown from one wall to the next. Lip and nose bloodied, The sound of my ribs cracking like dry twigs. Rough hands wrapped around my throat. And that laugh…his cruel laugh.

(JULIA ELIZABETH *gasping for breath.* LIBRANCE *laughs.*)

JULIA ELIZABETH:	CHORUS:
Please God, save me!	The Lord is my shepherd
	I shall not want.
	The Lord is my shepherd
	I shall not want.
	The Lord is my shepherd.

JULIA ELIZABETH: The world slowly dimming around me. Brought to my knees, everything around me fading except for those hands sapping me of my life… And just as I made my peace with meeting death.

(KOKUMA *raises the scissors high and brings it down… The* CHORUS *exhales.*)

JULIA ELIZABETH: The hands released their grasp of my throat.
Body crumpled atop me.
Blood. So much blood.
And there she stood… Panting…

CHORUS: That little brown skin girl.

JULIA ELIZABETH: That little brown skin grey eyed girl.
Dark crimson red soaked her hands, face and clothes.

The scissors stained in blood dropped from her hand…
Clattered against the floor beside the body of Mr
Librance.
Seemed like it almost echoed throughout the house.
Blood splattered her pretty face.
What was that in your eyes?

EAST: Fear,

WEST: Shock,

SOUTH: Rage,

NORTH: Joy…

CHORUS: There's joy on the girl's face.

JULIA ELIZABETH: "Come with me child. We must leave
this place."
I'll never be able to explain his death. No matter how
hard I tried.
The men of the Librance Family are cruel ones.
Far worse than my husband.
They'd never let me have this home or the property
that walked it…
I was ruined.
And my life they'd certainly take.
There was only one option.
"Child gather our things, only the essentials… only
what we can carry." I wipe my husband's blood from
her face…

MAWU: In the cold of night, they filled a wagon with
as much as they could carry, tethered an ugly spotted
horse to the wagon.

(MAWU *hands each of them a knapsack.*)

JULIA ELIZABETH: Pain still driving through my body,
My ribs… They… The pain. But I pushed forward. Few
things of food, some blankets, some clothes and an old
chest…filled with money and… A deed to some land.

If funds proved low I could sell that deed. Mr Librance never did trust the banks. I never thought his mistrust of banks would ever be useful…till now.

MAWU: Moon light guided them forward.

CHORUS: Northward.

JULIA ELIZABETH: I left that prison I once knew as home. Me and that grey eyed slave girl.

MAWU: Took to the road. Into the desolate countryside.

SOUTH: The road empty.

MAWU: Crossed the river, over a bridge.

(The lights shift and change.)

EAST: Drove til the night became day and then day became night again.

JULIA ELIZABETH: We can't travel much farther. We'll rest here. Get us a fire started. Start back up in the morning.

That sound alright to you Abigail?

Why am I talking to a mute?

MAWU: Settled the wagons in the woods just on the outskirts of the road.
Gathered some twigs and some branches.

JULIA ELIZABETH: Struggling to start the fire, I talked for I had no one else to talk to.

WEST: Spark.

JULIA ELIZABETH: I told her about Boston…
About pretty dresses and pretty parties.
Times I've longed missed.

EAST & NORTH: Spark.

JULIA ELIZABETH: I told her about my father.
How he gave my hand in marriage to a cruel drunkard of a man.

WEST, EAST, NORTH: Spark

JULIA ELIZABETH: I spoke of hopes and dreams beyond that of being a house wife ruined. How in a way I like that girl was a slave to the white man.

CHORUS: Spark, spark, spark…

JULIA ELIZABETH: Why won't this damn fire start?

KOKUMA: You talk too much.

JULIA ELIZABETH: What?

KOKUMA: You tell too many stories… You blow out fire before it starts with all your stories. Give here.
(She takes the flint.)
You see easy.

CHORUS: FIRE!

JULIA ELIZABETH: Dear God, you talk.

KOKUMA: Yes, yes, I talk, I talk your way good… More and more I learn to talk your words every night. You good teacher you never stop talking. You think I care about your fancy dances and your fancy dresses to please the white man. You no slave. Tell me this how many babies died crying and hungry because milk from mothers' breasts feed to Master's child? How many boys not allowed to become men? How many have been chained in cages of ships? How many have been whipped and beaten? How many have bled? How many have died? How many tears have mothers cried? How many mothers had their children ripped out of their hands? You don't know my pain. Never will. We not the same, we not the same at all. I'm still slave, you still mistress.

JULIA ELIZABETH: Abigail?

KOKUMA: And my name is not Abigail
Know this…
I enjoyed killing husband.

I enjoyed it great deal.
I loved it….

JULIA ELIZABETH: Why you little bitch of a girl… I've never been spoken to like that.

MAWU: Wrapped in blankets, they ate their meals and laid down for the night.
She feared whether she'd be killed in her sleep or whether the girl would leave her to fend for herself. That's what she feared the most. More than death by the Librance family hand, or whatever other horror could await them on this journey, but above all else, a fear of being alone. Julia moved between awake and dreaming.
Librance appears from the darkness, his hands bloody he looks first towards his blood-soaked hands and then towards Julia.

NORTH: (Appears as LIBRANCE) Julia…Julia dear,
Look what you've done to me.

JULIA ELIZABETH: Thomas?
Thomas is that you?

NORTH: Look at what you done, Julie dear.
You betrayed me…
Why did you betray me?

(Fades into the darkness)

MAWU: Julia tossed and turned in her sleep. The darkness wrapping around her like a blanket. As her heart pounded heavy in the cave of her chest.

KOKUMA: I woke as the sunrise peaked over the treelines. Mistress Julia still slept. I could leave her here, take the food and wagon before she wakes up… Or better yet kill her.

EAST: Kill her like you did her husband.

KOKUMA: Kill her like I did that evil man.

EAST: There's a rock right there.

KOKUMA: I could do it.

SOUTH: Kill her.

KOKUMA: Feel my hands and arms soaked with her warm blood up to the elbows. Bathe in it.

WEST: Kill her.

(KOKUMA *tests the heft of the rock.*)

KOKUMA: Rocks not too heavy.

EAST: Kill her.

KOKUMA: Have to hit her a few times to crack her skull.

CHORUS: KILL HER

KOKUMA: It'll be easy. Climb atop her.
Pin down her arms.
I'd have to swing hard.

SOUTH: This is the only way, Kokuma.

KOKUMA: She'll put up a fight.

CHORUS: Picture your mother. See her death.

(KOKUMA *raises the rock high above her head.*)

KOKUMA: This is the only way…this is the only way-

CHORUS: Kill her.
Kill her.
Kill her…

KOKUMA: Aaaaaahhhhh!!! I can't!
I'm sorry momma. I'm sorry.
I can't.
Part of me…part of me feels a sadness for her.
Part of me doesn't want to be alone in this strange land.

(*She tosses and turns in her blankets and coughs many times before she opened her eyes.*)

Get up, we must keep moving.

(KOKUMA *drops the rock in front of* JULIA ELIZABETH *and walks away.*)

MAWU: An hour later the two were on the road again. The roads were lonely seemed to stretch along for an eternity. Up steep hills and down valleys lo.

JULIA ELIZABETH: Let's stop for a few.

KOKUMA: Why Mistress?

JULIA ELIZABETH: We should stop here. Just for a few.

KOKUMA: It's not yet night time.

JULIA ELIZABETH: I said we stop here damnit!

MAWU: Silence.

(JULIA ELIZABETH *coughs. Coughs hard. She collapses to her knees holding her side.*)

KOKUMA: Mistress? Mistress are you good?

JULIA ELIZABETH: Like she cared.
Like she gave a damn if I coughed my lung out, collapsed right then and there and died. (*She calms herself, icy calm*) You understand this, child. When I say we go, we go. When I saw we stop, we stop.
Do you understand me?
(*Silence*)
Oh no child. You can't fake that you don't have a tongue now. I asked if you understood me?
(*Silence*)

KOKUMA: Yes mistress.

JULIA ELIZABETH: Good. Let us continue on.

JULIA ELIZABETH / KOKUMA: Bitch.

(MAWU *bangs her staff against the ground three times…*)

(JULIA ELIZABETH *and* KOKUMA *pause, size each other up, huff in exasperation.*)

(Again MAWU *bangs her staff against the ground three times… The two continue on their journey.)*

CHORUS: Days stretch on.

MAWU: The body of Mr Librance, and the disappearance of Julia and her slave had been discover long before then. Holden Librance the patriarch of the family didn't take kindly to the knowledge his sons life had been taken by a woman. Didn't matter whether it was white or negra, he was going to get his revenge he swore. Sent his last two remaining sons Junior and Pearson along with six good men and six bloodhound to fetch them, answers had to be given and soon.

*(*NORTH *and* SOUTH *transform into Junior and Pearson Librance.)*

NORTH: *(As* JUNIOR*)* I never liked my brother dear, but a transgression against the family is still a transgression.
Father sent us cause he knew my brother and I had become renown during our youth, we became known as men that managed to get things done. Truth be told, certain events during our youth made us quite respected and feared amongst the community.

(Pearson giggles…)

SOUTH: *(As Pearson)* Tell them about the pig.

NORTH: Now now I'm getting to it. Now me and Pearson took this pregnant woman up to hill over at Buckley's Point. Tied her up to an old tree.

SOUTH: Cut her open real good.
Pearson giggled after he finished.

NORTH: These could have been a surgeons hands… Just out curiosity and tad bit of sportin' fun…We decided to cut open her belly, yanked out the unborn child and put a piglet inside her. Sewed her up nice tight like a

stuffed turkey and sat there for two days just to watch
as the pig scratched and bit it's way on out.

SOUTH: Sure was a sight to see.

NORTH: Yeah we watched as we drank whiskey
and lemonade stolen from our fathers office, eating
sandwiches and we watched…

SOUTH: They were turkey sandwiches.

NORTH: Watched…as that negress tether back and
forth on the shaky boundary between living and the
great beyond inbetween the entire time,

SOUTH: Screaming and crying…

NORTH: Yes brother, we watch as she was screaming
and crying, begging to be joined with her unborn.
But enough reminiscin' on memories of old we got a
task at hand and run-away bride to bring back home.

WEST: But Julia and Kokuma had other things to worry
about other than the cruelities of men.

MAWU: For America can be just as cruel.

JULIA ELIZABETH: I began to wish we had killed my
husband during the summer months.

CHORUS: The winter was hard.

NORTH: They travel through countryside and cities.

WEST: Money started dwindling…

EAST: Same with food.

NORTH: Only thing on their minds…

KOKUMA / JULIA ELIZABETH: Survival.

SOUTH / WEST: Travel… Eat… Sleep…

NORTH / EAST: Travel… Eat… Sleep…

EAST: Sleep some nights interrupted by the grumbles in
their bellies… other nights they would…

WEST: Tossed and turned in their sleeps dreaming of the horror they've witnessed in their lifetimes.

NORTH: In every dream Kokuma would see the face of her mother's killer, slowly change into that of Mr Librance. Eyes hollowed, his mouth gaping open, blood trickling out, face rotting.

CHORUS: She'd call out in her dreams.

KOKUMA: Mother Moon…Mother Moon… Can you hear me?

MAWU: I hear you child, I'm here.

KOKUMA: Please Mother Moon, how much longer must we wander through this evil land, how much longer must I carry these nightmares?
Even when I sleep I see the ghosts of my family.
The face of those who stole me away…
Stop these nightmares.
You said you'd get me to freedom…

MAWU: I will soon child, but you must be patient. The road to freedom will be a hard one, child.

KOKUMA: And these nightmares?

MAWU: I wish I could help you un-see the horrors you've witnessed, my child. Just know I'm with you.

KOKUMA: What good is that to me?

MAWU: Kokuma…

KOKUMA: No… No… No more…you say you are with me, but what good does it do me?
You know what you have taught me?
That I can't depend on you or any other gods or spirits.
You have taught me that if I'm to survive this world then I must do it by myself.

MAWU: You don't mean that?

KOKUMA: I do. I do very much so.

You. Leave. Me.
I don't need or want your help no more.
Go! Go away and don't come back.

(MAWU *fades away into the darkness.*)

WEST: Morning came followed by another and another.

EAST: Florence, South Carolina

WEST: To Bennettsville

SOUTH: Outskirts of Asheboro on up to the Roanoke River

NORTH: In a small little town not far from the river…

SOUTH: Tacked onto the wall of the post office…

JULIA ELIZABETH: There we saw it.

KOKUMA: It's you. It's your face.
What does it read?

JULIA ELIZABETH: It read that I was…

CHORUS: Missing.

JULIA ELIZABETH: Not wanted for murder nor for theft… Just…

CHORUS: Missing.

JULIA ELIZABETH: Like a white woman in this day in age couldn't rage in her heart… Couldn't be capable of using employing violence upon a man… Part of me felt… Part of me was grateful that I was not wanted for murder, but deep within me… Deep in a corner of my soul it churned with a aching…this fire…an anger…
Is that all I am just a woman? Just a woman that too demur? Too small?
No no no…if the world only knew the atrocities…the crimes…the pitch blackness I bottled in same as any man. Same as any woman. There's more to me than just a woman. I don't need to be saved. I wanted to scream.

KOKUMA: It means trouble, the thing that this reads?

(JULIA ELIZABETH *exhales.*)

KOKUMA: I rip the poster off the wall.
We must go?

JULIA ELIZABETH: Yes, we must go.

CHORUS: Traveled and traveled…

JULIA ELIZABETH: The Lord is my shepherd, I shall not want…
The Lord is my shepherd, I shall not want…
The Lord is my shepherd, I shall not want…
Bound for Boston. Finally heading home. Home…
Home to father. The man that sold me.
Will he accept me back? I didn't care… God was guiding me home.
Well will you look at that. Abigail take a look at that, will you.
This is hill country. Have to love the hill country.
Beautiful isn't it?

KOKUMA: I don't care for your evil land.

JULIA ELIZABETH: There's nothing evil about this place, this is God's country.

KOKUMA: You're God is evil too.

JULIA ELIZABETH: Now wait a minute child. You can speak bad about many things but don't talk about my religion. You don't see me talking bad about your heathen faith.

KOKUMA: What good has your Christian God done?

JULIA ELIZABETH: My God has taken you out of your land of paganism and savagery and showed you Christian love, child. My God has given you--

KOKUMA: My land was a place of love… It was a small little fishing village… A land of peace. It was

your land. Your land that has shown me nothing but
savagery. Your people are nothing but savages.

JULIA ELIZABETH: I'm the savage?
You call me a savage.

KOKUMA: Who stole me away from my home?
Who chained me in ship?
Who steal my name, give me name that not my own?

JULIA ELIZABETH: You ungrateful girl.
You think I like sleeping in the dirt?
If I was such a damn dirty savage, then I would have
gone about my own business and let that devil of a
man have his way with you but instead I put my body,
my life, and my livelihood in harm's way for you…
And you have the audacity to call me a savage.

KOKUMA: Who is to say he didn't already?

JULIA ELIZABETH: What?

KOKUMA: Who is to say he didn't already… Have his…
Have his way with me.

JULIA ELIZABETH: You are lying.

KOKUMA: Who is to say he didn't already lay atop me.

Who is to say he didn't already touch me here, and
here, and here, and here, and here, and here, and
here!!!

JULIA ELIZABETH: Shut up!

KOKUMA: Left me upstairs bruised, hurting, and
bleeding all while you drink your fancy teas and wear
your fancy clothes laughing and laughing downstairs
with your fancy ladies.
Who is to say I'm not carrying his seed in my belly
right now?

JULIA ELIZABETH: I don't know why you'd say such a
filthy lie.

I should have let him ravage you.

KOKUMA: And I should have let him take your life.
Who is the savage here, now?

(JULIA ELIZABETH *raises her hand and slaps* KOKUMA.)

JULIA ELIZABETH: Oh my god… Oh my god… Abigail.

KOKUMA: Don't touch me.
Don't ever touch me!

(JULIA ELIZABETH *watches as* KOKUMA *runs off.*)

JULIA ELIZABETH: Abigail…Abigail come back this is
hard mean country, this is not a place for a child like
you to be wandering off in.
Come back.
Oh what did I do?
What did I do?
Every fiber in my being wishes that I could take
that moment back. I heard her crying in the woods
somewhere. Crying pain-filled tears, I wanted to go to
her. I should apologize…I should comfort her…no…
no…I should leave… Damn the girl…I should leave
without her but…I couldn't… No matter how many
times my brain said leave, my heart said-

(KOKUMA *in the woods. She's crying…*)

(*Beats upon her stomach*)

(*The* WINDS *begin to dance around her.*)

KOKUMA: Mother Moon.
Mother Moon.
Show your self to me.
I don't want this child.
I don't want this life.
I don't want this.
Take it away.

(KOKUMA *screams and as she does the winds lift her high and then cradles her in her arms quieting her. They hum to her til she falls asleep.*)

CHORUS: Finally after what seemed like an eternity she came out.

WEST: They slept by the camp fire hungry for warmth on that cold and miserable winter night.

SOUTH: They slept apart from each other that night and when the sun rose again their wagon hitched, they traveled hard.

KOKUMA: We had lost time to make up for.

CHORUS: After three nights of silence …

JULIA ELIZABETH: I…I shouldn't have struck you.

KOKUMA: No… No you should not.

JULIA ELIZABETH: I'm not pleased with myself for doing it, child.
It was very unladylike of me.

KOKUMA: And…

JULIA ELIZABETH: I won't strike out at you again like that.
I promise. Can we be…
Can we be civil to one another?

KOKUMA: Civil?

JULIA ELIZABETH: It means…nice to one another. We have a long journey ahead of us and a hard one. It makes no sense to be at each others throats when we have such a long way to go. Can we do that? Can we be polite?

KOKUMA: Yes… We can be polite. We can be…civil.

JULIA ELIZABETH: As we journeyed the swamp country, one wheel of our wagon broke.

KOKUMA: We unpacked what we could.

JULIA ELIZABETH: Took only what we could carry.

KOKUMA: What I could carry.

JULIA ELIZABETH: We emptied the contents of the trunk into a burlap bag. Saddled it to our horse.

KOKUMA: Walked on in silence as the snow began to drift down upon the muddy path,
Our horse struggled through the swampland roads.

(The sound of thunder)

JULIA ELIZABETH: Trudged forward for quite awhile before Abigail stopped us

KOKUMA: Walked on in silence as the snow began to drift down upon the muddy path,
Our horse struggled through the swampland roads.

(The sound of thunder)

KOKUMA: Listen.

JULIA ELIZABETH: I heard nothing.

KOKUMA: Listen closer.

(The sound of thunder fills the air.)

JULIA ELIZABETH: There it was… we heard in the distance the sound of galloping horses and barking dogs.

KOKUMA: Closer and closer they seemed to grow.

JULIA ELIZABETH: We turned to see two riders followed by six other.
I recognized those faces immediately.
And they recognized me.
Pearson and Junior.

KOKUMA: Trouble

CHORUS: Death on horseback.

JULIA ELIZABETH: Climbed onto the horse.

KOKUMA: The fear in her eyes was the same as that of my mother's before she died-

JULIA ELIZABETH: We must run child. Give me your hand.

KOKUMA: Although it wasn't the language of my people, for some reason fear always sounds the same.

JULIA ELIZABETH: Pulled that girl onto the saddle. Rode hard. Fast.
This was a cart pulling horse, it wasn't made for running hard.
Let alone carry two on its back…

(MAWU *appears and lifts her staff high.*)

JULIA ELIZABETH: But it moved.
Away from our pursuers.
Weaving through trees and deeper into the swamp country.
If they found us. Captured us. Lord knows what they'd do to the girl… To me.
I know this much for certain, I didn't want to find out.
We pushed onward until finally we could hide ourselves away… Breathe.

KOKUMA: Who were those men?
Who were those men chasing us?
Are they cruel men?

JULIA ELIZABETH: Yes dear, those are cruel men…those men are savages. And we must stay off the main roads if we have any hopes of surviving. Stay clear away from those men. You understand me, girl?

KOKUMA: I do.

JULIA ELIZABETH: Good… Good… We should get some rest. Don't start a fire tonight. We don't want them seeing us in the darkness. We have a long hard journey ahead of us.

MAWU: That night as they huddled together in the cold and in the darkness. Julia Elizabeth sat there, cradling the young girl in her arms, staring upward at the sky. In her mind she named the constellations which her father once sat her upon his knees and taught her their names. She couldn't go to Boston no longer, the Librance brothers would be looking for her there. Options for safety where slipping away from her and the feeling of homelessness and loneliness took over her very soul. Thoughts of ways to get out of this situation filled her mind as numerous as there were stars about in the night sky.

NORTH: Big Dipper

EAST: Cassiopeia

WEST: Orion.

SOUTH: Lupus

MAWU: A gentle breeze stirred the air, and Kokuma let out a moan in her sleep.

CHORUS: The ghosts of her ancestors called to her.

SOUTH: But for Julia Elizabeth, the thoughts stirred, and stirred in her mind, She could leave her. She could leave her here to find a way to escape. She could give them the girl. She could tell them who really killed Mr. Librance, she could come back home once again.

EAST: Go back to the life of her launder clothes, soft beds, and a full belly. The taste of wine, roasted chicken, and sweet cakes…the aroma of coffee and music…oh how she missed the sound of music filling her home when she was entertaining and meaningless conversations. She was certain even the poor girl dreamed of going back to that life. She wouldn't fault her for giving her up…

JULIA ELIZABETH: She'd understand.
She'd have to understand.

CHORUS: No…no…a new thought stirred and stirred in her mind.

NORTH: She could continue on without the girl.

WEST: The girl that was slowing her down.

EAST: The girl that had once wished her death.

JULIA ELIZABETH: I could kill her. Leave her here. Throw them off my path. They're looking for me and the negra girl. Not me on my own.

NORTH: Or…

CHORUS: We could kill her now.

EAST: It would be the humane thing to do to end the girl's misery here.

JULIA ELIZABETH: But how?

EAST: The scissors.

SOUTH: We can end her life with the scissors.

NORTH: Poetic almost.

JULIA ELIZABETH: But does it have to be done like that?

EAST: We can make it quick.

SOUTH: She won't suffer.

NORTH: Stab and cut into her throat.

CHORUS: Twist…

WEST: Kill her like she did your husband.

MAWU: But as quickly as the idea passes through her mind, Sssshhh…

JULIA ELIZABETH: It's gone.
It'll be alright…
We'll be alright…I'll be alright…

CHORUS: The scissors rested in her pocket.

(JULIA ELIZABETH *coughs. Coughs. Coughs hard*)

MAWU: In the morning cold damp fog covered them as they journeyed.

EAST: Stayed in the wood, but followed the road.

WEST: Day became night.

EAST: Night became day.

WEST: And back again.

MAWU: The fog seemed to follow them on their journey.

EAST: Feet sore. Blistered and bloodied.

WEST: Stomachs empty.

NORTH: The winter cold slapping them.

SOUTH: As they journeyed through the haze.

KOKUMA: We came upon a wagon full of provisions and a short way beyond that was two men huddled by a camp fire, singing Christians hymns as they drank and roasted a rabbit over a spit. The darkness and the fog seemed to part from them.
Mistress we should continue on. We should go around them.

JULIA ELIZABETH: Not everyone is Mr Librance.

KOKUMA: Mistress we should go. I don't like the feeling of this.

JULIA ELIZABETH: Nonsense child. They have food and a warm fire. And listen their singing…these aren't the ones chasing us. These are good Christian men. Come on now. Let me do all the talking.

KOKUMA: You're trust in Christian Men to be Christian, scares me.

She moved forward and I followed. They were dirty looking men.

JULIA ELIZABETH: Hello there gentlemen.

EAST: Hello.

JULIA ELIZABETH: Me and my girl, have been travelling quite awhile, our wagon broke down along the journey. May we rest here by your fire.

WEST: Wouldn't be right Christian, to turn away a woman in need now would it.
Suppose ya'll can rest with us a bit.

JULIA ELIZABETH: Thank you. I'm Julia Elizabeth and this is my girl Abigail.

WEST: Me myself I go by the name Pence. This man over there they call Bonaparte.

EAST: Good evening, ma'am.

WEST: Can we interest you in a bit of our rabbit? It ain't much but what is ours is yours. Suppose your girl can eat as well.

JULIA ELIZABETH: That's would be kind of you.

EAST: We got us some wine as well.

WEST: Where you headed?

JULIA ELIZABETH: Boston. To... visit my family.

EAST: Long journey ahead of you.

JULIA ELIZABETH: We do indeed.

WEST: I hope you don't mind me saying this but for the life of me I can't place it but you look familiar to me.

JULIA ELIZABETH: I don't know.

KOKUMA: We ate our rabbit in silence, listening to the men revel in stories of drunken festivities and raunchy jokes.

WEST: Eh… Eh… Eh… What's the difference between a dog and a fox?

EAST: I don't know, what?

WEST: About three drinks.

KOKUMA: Hmph… These were Christian men.
And once the food and drink was consumed and the fire light started to burn low.

JULIA ELIZABETH: Well thank you gentlemen for your hospitality.
We're most grateful for your kindness.

EAST: You're leaving?

JULIA ELIZABETH: We really should be on our way. We have quite a long journey ahead of us still.

EAST: So you just gonna eat up our food and go? That sound right to you Pence?

WEST: Not at all.

EAST: You ask me you take in this world, you gotta give.

WEST: Sounds about right to me.

JULIA ELIZABETH: We don't have anything to give.

WEST: Well you better think of something mighty quick.

EAST: This is after all…what's the word?

WEST: Capitalistic

EAST: A capitalistic society we live in. Land of give and take.

KOKUMA: Why do you never listen to me?

JULIA ELIZABETH: I thought you were Christians…

WEST: Oh we are.

EAST: But we're Americans first. Some kind of a trade or an exchange must come our way.

WEST: Jesus helps those, who help themselves.

JULIA ELIZABETH: I'll give you my wedding ring. It'll fetch you a good price.

WEST: What a ring gonna do for us?

EAST: What we gonna do. Marry the mule.

WEST: Oh that's a good one.

EAST: Thank you... thank you very much.

JULIA ELIZABETH: I have nothing to give.

EAST: Oh no, you are a woman, you got plenty to give.

WEST: Bet you give real good too.

EAST: I'm sure she does.

JULIA ELIZABETH: You can have Abigail.

KOKUMA: What?

JULIA ELIZABETH: You can have my girl.

KOKUMA: Mistress, what are you saying?

JULIA ELIZABETH: My husband paid a good amount of money for her. She's a hard worker. Knows her way around the duties of the house, She's of breeding age. And won't give too much trouble when spoken too.

EAST: We know how to deal with troublemakers, don't we?

WEST: Got the cuts on my hands from tying all those nooses to prove it.

KOKUMA: Mistress?!!

JULIA ELIZABETH: She can cook, clean, mend your clothes, satisfy whatever your needs and wants might be. As you said we live in America. But I give up the girl. You give me a week's worth of food and provisions, and one of them mules you have.

WEST: One of the mules?

JULIA ELIZABETH: Can you lay with a mule?

EAST: Why can't we just have our way with them both?

WEST: Come on now Bonaparte we're not heathen. This is business. Mule and half of week, now that sounds like a fair exchange to me.

JULIA ELIZABETH: The mule and half a week of provisions. That's more than fair.

(MAWU *begins to dance. A wild frentic dance*)

(*The remaining winds churn around her.*)

KOKUMA: Mistress what are you doing?
Mistress what did you do?
Mistress what is happening?
Why are you doing this mistress?
Don't do this.
Don't let them take me! Don't let them take me!

(EAST *and* WEST *prepare to carry the girl away with them.*)

(MAWU *bangs her staff to the ground three times.*)

JULIA ELIZABETH: Stop!!!
I change my mind. Take back the provisions and the food. Take back the mule.

EAST: A deal is a deal.

JULIA ELIZABETH: I'll…I'll make another deal. I have a deed to some land.

EAST: We're travelling folks what we want with a deed.

JULIA ELIZABETH: You can… You can have your way with me. Just… Just give me back the girl.

EAST: Look at you just sweetening the deal.

WEST: Ah wait a minute…I have seen you. You that woman on that missing poster.

MAWU: Kokuma!

(MAWU *hands* KOKUMA *her staff.*)

KOKUMA: When they aren't paying attention I see a thick branch on the ground, I pick it up and…

(KOKUMA *fights, she fights hard, moves she didn't know she knew, the staff raised high, she fought them as if possessed by a warriors spirit and beats the two men unconscious, in surprise at herself she drops the staff.*)

JULIA ELIZABETH: How did you do that?

(KOKUMA *looks down at her hands in shock and back at* JULIA ELIZABETH *before picking it back up turning the staff upon her.*)

KOKUMA: You were going to give me to those dirty men.

JULIA ELIZABETH: No Abigail.

KOKUMA: Don't lie.
You were going to give me to those men, for what? Badly cooked rabbit and a mule.
I should…I should beat you like I did those men.

JULIA ELIZABETH: Abigail?

KOKUMA: My name is Kokuma, daughter of the high priestess, the blood of the first woman kissed by Mother Moon runs through my veins. I am the moon's chosen.

JULIA ELIZABETH: You can't leave me.
Please don't…don't leave me.

KOKUMA: How dare you tell me what I can do now… Don't you dare try to betray me again.

JULIA ELIZABETH: I won't…I promise I'll never do that again…I'm sorry. I'm sorry I was afraid.

KOKUMA: You spineless woman. May your ancestors curse you for your cowardice. When the time comes for your heart to prove its courage, I hope you find it. We continued on.

CHORUS: They continued one.

KOKUMA: It's the damp that chills you.

JULIA ELIZABETH: Couldn't see what was behind us.

KOKUMA: Couldn't see what was in front of us.

EAST: They shivered in the wind.

WEST: Everything smelled of damp and rot.

KOKUMA: That was the stench of the land called America.

MAWU: The winds pushed Julia Elizabeth and Kokuma forward through the cold mist…

WEST: Rain fell

EAST: Turned to cold sleet

CHORUS: Sleet into snow.

SOUTH: Ashy grey covered this cruel land.

MAWU: They travelled onward. The winds gusted hard. A hundred crows circled overhead.

JULIA ELIZABETH: And then as we trudged through that lonely place. Abigail stopped in her tracks, looked upwards and let out a gasp.

KOKUMA: Twenty five bodies.

CHORUS: Black bodies.

NORTH: Men

WEST: Women

EAST: Children

KOKUMA: My heart shattered into shards in that place, and was scattered by the wind. Twenty five black bodies, hands tied behind their backs, burned beyond recognition, swinging from their necks, faces frozen by the cold winds in an appearance of eternal horror. They hung upon those trees moving in a slow funeral dance in the air.

(CHORUS *changes into the hanged bodies, they swing from the branches. Humming a death song*)

JULIA ELIZABETH: Abigail's staggered forward, her legs gave out from under her.

KOKUMA: Why would someone do something like this?

JULIA ELIZABETH: They must have done something wrong, to deserve a fate like that.

KOKUMA: Must have done something wrong? Must have done something wrong?!!!
AAAAAHHH!!! THIS EVIL LAND, THIS PLACE YOU CALL AMERICA!!!

JULIA ELIZABETH: Silence child.
Silence whoever did this could be still around.
Do you want them to hear us?

KOKUMA: I don't care. What kind of a land do you live in where this good? Where the blood of innocents can be spilled for no reason and its their fault? What kind of land is this where we see the innocent killed and we say this is their fault. You tell me that?!!! Why is this land filled with such heartless people?

JULIA ELIZABETH: Abigail. Abigail? What are you doing?

KOKUMA: I'm cutting them down!

JULIA ELIZABETH: You can't.

KOKUMA: YES I CAN! I may be a slave but I will free them.

JULIA ELIZABETH: Abigail we must go.

KOKUMA: Go then.

JULIA ELIZABETH: I'm leaving. Abigail, this isn't our…
We shouldn't concern ourselves with this. I'm going.

KOKUMA: Go.

JULIA ELIZABETH: I'm leaving right now.
I'm leaving without you.
Abigail, I swear it I'm leaving you.

KOKUMA: If you are going to go, then go.
But if you are going to stay then.
Help me then to do something that is right.
(She begins to cut them one by one.)

(Silence)

JULIA ELIZABETH: I don't know why but I helped her
cut one by one those bodies from the trees.

KOKUMA: Help me. Help me please. I need you.

(Silence)

JULIA ELIZABETH: I don't know why but I helped her
cut one by one those bodies from the trees.

*(KOKUMA and JULIA ELIZABETH take down each of the
bodies one by one. Lay them next to each other.)*

KOKUMA: Using some wet planks we found alongside
the road so we can dig a shallow grave, we struggle to
break through the frozen soil, our hands blistered and
sore, and just when we couldn't dig anymore…

(MAWU raises her staff and bangs it three times.)

KOKUMA: The bodies rise up, stand tall, heads held
high…and walked…no…they drifted like snowflakes
into their graves, and snow covered the bodies before
the dirt could.

JULIA ELIZABETH: We stood in silence.
Did you see what I just saw?

KOKUMA: I did.

(*Silence. Long silence*)

JULIA ELIZABETH: We speak of this to no one they'd think us mad.

Agreed?

KOKUMA: Agreed.

JULIA ELIZABETH: Come here child... Come here.

(KOKUMA *approaches* JULIA ELIZABETH.)

KOKUMA: What?

JULIA ELIZABETH: Don't what me child, come here.
Let me see your hands.
Ah they'll be no good to you soon dear, if we don't get them tended to. Liable they'll get infected and you wind up sick. No use for travelling with you like that.
Let's get that taken care shall we?

(JULIA ELIZABETH *rips the hem from her dress, wraps it around* KOKUMA's *hands, makes a gauze.*)

KOKUMA: How'd you learn this?

JULIA ELIZABETH: My mother.

KOKUMA: Your mother taught you?

JULIA ELIZABETH: My mother, same woman that gave me this brooch right here, she was a healer...
I'd pick up a thing here and there when I wasn't learning about fancy dances and fancy dresses.

(*Silence*)

KOKUMA: Thank you.

JULIA ELIZABETH: It's nothing dear.

KOKUMA: No...thank you for helping me cut them down and bury them.
Why did you stay? Why did you help me?

(Silence)

JULIA ELIZABETH: We should travel on, child.
We must go.

CHORUS: They travelled on.

NORTH: Tracked through the cruel weather.

KOKUMA & JULIA ELIZABETH: Moved forward

WEST: Pushed on

*(JULIA ELIZABETH and KOKUMA journey onward.
KOKUMA carries the burlap sack.)*

KOKUMA: We passed towns with more churches than
houses.

CHORUS: Journeyed on.

KOKUMA: Every road we travelled snow kissed its
muddy ground.

CHORUS: We journeyed on.

KOKUMA: The land barren, seemed to sneer at us as we
travelled across its face. Snow started to fall again.

CHORUS: Still we journeyed on.

*(EAST transforms in that moment in to the Man named
Scratch.)*

EAST: *(Sings)*
Let me tell you a story
That's simple and true…
Of an angel
Thrown down to earth
Became a snake wrapped around that life tree
On your soul he feeds
The devil that's me.
That's the devil that's me.

KOKUMA: Crossed a bridge that stretched over an
angry rapid, and there on the other side wrapped in
blankets a man sat. Guitar in hand strumming and a

funny little hat on his head. His skin like… Mine. Snow as it fell before it could even rest upon him seemed to smoke and sizzle.

EAST: Oh well hello there ladies, what are you doing on a chilly afternoon like this.

JULIA ELIZABETH: You there. Boy. Is there a town or inn nearby. We need some food and warmth before we continue our travels.

EAST: Now ma'am, I don't see no boy in sight, what ya see standin'…is one that goes by the name of Scratch, some folks call me Little Horn. But I assure ya there is nothing little about me.

JULIA ELIZABETH: I beg your pardon.

EAST: Oh, Sorry didn't mean to offend. That's jus' how I speak now and again. Lord forgive me.

JULIA ELIZABETH: Where's your masters, boy?

EAST: Massas? Massas she says, ha! Nobody want no old devil like me. I make too much trouble for 'em, people say I'm too much damn trouble for them. Folks like me, in this land if they can't make money off ya, then they either kill or leave alone to me business. But they let me alone and let me preach the word, sometimes we find ways to get along in this world… most time we don't.

JULIA ELIZABETH: I see.

EAST: Do ya really though?

JULIA ELIZABETH: Do I really what?

EAST: Nuthin' missus…the lil' one will learn what I'm sayin' soon enuff if she don't already…I reckon.

KOKUMA: He winked and smiled my direction. His smile wider and more frightening than the wildest of rivers.

EAST: If ya lookin' for some food and some warmth, let me take ya on down to this nice folks down the way. Good ole christian white folks good natured sort. They'd take to ya'll kindly. Follow me, I'll take ya'll there, follow me.

KOKUMA: Scratch, gathered up his things and motioned with his head for them to follow, which they did, keeping back a few steps. Lead us through a strange mist. A thick mist that blinded us and choked us on our journey before we made it to a small shack. Beaten from time. Soft yellow light from a fire inside the house and greeted us. The door opened as we approached. An elderly man and a woman appeared. Their skins stretched over their bones when they smiled.

JULIA ELIZABETH: But it was the first welcoming smile we've seen in such a long time.

KOKUMA: They welcome us into their home.

EAST: I brought ya some sweet tings' for ya evenin' supper.

(WEST and SOUTH *take on the role of the old couple.*

WEST: Well don't you two look just scrumptious.

SOUTH: Absolutely delicious.

WEST: Come on in…come on in…

SOUTH: Set yourself on over at the table over here, honey. Are ya'll hungry?

JULIA ELIZABETH: Thank you so much. Been so long since we've met kindness.

WEST: Oh anybody that ole' devil brings by is welcomed in this house.

EAST: Mind if I speak with ya young girl? Come with me child.

KOKUMA: Come with him I did. Out into the darkness that surrounded that old shack. I watched as he lit his pipe.

JULIA ELIZABETH: I want to thank you for taking us in. Been so long since we've meet kindness.

WEST: What's this world without a little Christian charity?

JULIA ELIZABETH: Placed down before me a warm bowl of stew.
Oh this looks heavenly.

SOUTH: Well then eat up, child.

(JULIA ELIZABETH *raises the spoon up.*)

EAST: You like dat white woman ya walkin' wit?

KOKUMA: She's alright to me.

EAST: Alright to you, huh?
What if I told ya I have a way for you to be rid of her? She can't be dat good to ya.
So what if I could free you from her? What if I told you, I have me ways of getting' you to freedom wit outta dat woman? It could be done.

KOKUMA: What do you mean by this?

JULIA ELIZABETH: Maybe I should wait for Abigail to join me?
(*She puts the spoon down.*)

SOUTH & WEST: Eat child.

WEST: She'll be along soon.

SOUTH: You don't want your food to grow cold.

(JULIA ELIZABETH *raises her spoon to her mouth but stops herself.*)

JULIA ELIZABETH: Where are my manners? Won't you be joining me.

SOUTH: We'll eat later, love.

SOUTH & WEST: Eat up.

(JULIA ELIZABETH *raises her spoon to her mouth.*)

EAST: Child…what do ya care about some white
woman? What dat white woman care 'bout ya? Now…
right now…there's a price on dat woman. Pretty pretty
price. You could be free of her. You can be free of her
right now. Split it three ways.

KOKUMA: Three ways?

EAST: Me, ya, the old couple. Ya can be rich. We all can
be rich.

KOKUMA: I don't know…

(EAST *loses the accent. His voice hardens.*)

EAST: Listen to me… You think if someone catches
you two together she won't throw you to the wolves?
Think she won't feed you to those that hunger for
blood? Hasn't she tried it once before? You could be
rid of her before she rid of you. I look at you and know
that you come from a people who were givers. But
know this…this land…these people…they will never
care about you child. It's just not in their nature. They
take…take from the land, take from your body…they
take from your soul if you let them. These people.
Oh these people… Your kind Julia Elizabeth in the
bunch as well… Speaks to me and calls me boy. Me
who watched The Great Father stretch the sky above
and place the sun and the moon in its home. Me who
watched as the first of man that was shaped with spit
and clay slithered from the muck…
She calls me a boy… Me who watched The Great
Father give dominion of this earth to man with such
pride, only to turn his back upon it in disgust. These
people…these people like Julia. They no better than
you…you who has been kissed by the sun and the

moon, and who have the night sky weaved into you skin. You who have the universe coursing through your blood. Yet they rule this land. Look at them… They are good at what they do… They act witty and kind. Appreciative of your love and your goodness… but at their core they are as cruel as this land… Nothing more than troubles… And we'll pay ya nicely as we help get rid of ya singular troubles. Cause that's what her kind is. Trust me…ya gonna want to walk this earth without her than have her by ya side. That's the only way you'll survive this new world.

KOKUMA: She's not like them… She's not like the rest of them.

EAST: Is that so? Ya know that for sure? I'm givin' ya a way to freedom. Say yes… Be a good girl and say yes. Say yes Kokuma.

KOKUMA: How… How do you know my name?

EAST: I know many things Kokuma. I know many things. I can't help it. Everything that shifts and moves round upon this hated earth I know. I know that you are special, precious, treasured… Blessed. Tell me this have you forgotten about your beautiful mother? Have you left your mother's cold and lifeless body rotting in the charred remains of that village and replaced her with that white woman?

KOKUMA: I would never!

EAST: What would she think little Kokuma? What would your mother think knowing that you left her behind, knowing that you've forgotten all about her?

KOKUMA: I haven't

EAST: Want to sit by the fire as your father sings to you and your mother… your precious mother… your beautiful mother holds you close and combs your hair. I can give you what you desire. I can give you everything you've wanted. Anything you want precious Kokuma. Look into my eyes and see…

KOKUMA: He puffs from his pipe…
The delicious smell of sukuma wiki fills my nostrils…
He puffs again and…
I can hear the waves crash against the ocean, the crackle of the fire, laughter and joy, I feel the heat followed by the cooling breeze that only my home can give me. My home…I look down and instead of snow there is the red brown soil under my feet…
The man smiles takes another puff from his pipe
And there in the haze I see motioning for me…
Baba?!!!

WEST: *(As her father)* My child. My child is that you?

KOKUMA: Can I speak to her? Will she hear me?

EAST: Anything your heart desires…

KOKUMA: Baba? It's my Father.

WEST: I've missed you…

KOKUMA: I've missed you so much Baba.

WEST: Come to me, my child. Join me here?

KOKUMA: Oh Baba, it's been so hard without you. I've missed you. I'm sorry. I never told you but it was me that blew out the holy fire. This is my fault that this has happened. It's my fault. Everything has been taken from me. I'm so sorry. I don't want to be in this cruel place no longer. I don't want to be in a world without my Baba and Yeye! I've failed you. I've failed the village. I've failed the ancestors and the spirits. It's my fault…it's my fault…it's my fault…
What do you need from me, Mister Scratch? Whatever you need from me I'll do. I just want to be with them.

(EAST *takes pity upon* KOKUMA.)

EAST: Oh this curse called principles…
Hush that talk, Kokuma, hush. As much as I'd love to
add you to my collection…I can't let a child believe the
evils of the world are on her. Look at me child. Just like
you pray to the mother moon, the white man's god is
death. The world is filled with evil and you can't place
that burden upon yourself. Know that your mother
and father loved you. Know that the holy fire of the
village burns inside of you, keep that flame burning.
Keep it burning for them, you hear me now? And
whatever happens, ya stay strong. Ya keep breathing.
Ya hear me? Here I want ya to have this here. Come
on…take this right here.

(EAST *hands* KOKUMA *a small leather pouch.*)

KOKUMA: What's this?

MAWU: Ya just hold on to it. Hold on to it and don't
open it until ya find yourself in a situation ya feel
there's no way out. Til ya feel like all hope is lost. Kept
me safe for a long time, more times than I can count.
Think it'll do the same for ya.

KOKUMA: Yes, ma'am.

MAWU: Good. Hold on to it. Hold on to it tight now.
You take care of yourself. You change your mind about
that white woman just look for me.

KOKUMA: Look for you where shall I find you?

EAST: I'll be on the crossroads, lil' grey eyed one.

KOKUMA: Scratch blew from his pipe, snapped his
fingers and…

EAST: And just like that…

(MAWU *and the* WINDS *snaps their finger.*)

(*Lights shift and change.*)

(*The shack and the fog disappears.*)

MAWU: They found themselves standing out underneath the night sky. The tiny weather-beaten shack, the elderly couple, old man Scratch, the delicious bowls of food in the bowl…all gone. They stood alone, the snow fell, and the winds howled. The sunlight slowly trickled out from the woods and found itself replaced by the moonlight.

CHORUS: Moonlight guided their every steps through the trees.

KOKUMA: Strange how even after witnessing the evil of men, the world continues on.
Night become day… Day into night.
The sun and the moon still rises and falls.
What's a life of a mortal to the moon?
Does she even care?

JULIA ELIZABETH: The silence on our walk after the horror we witnessed unbearable. But what was there this white woman could say to her? Or her to me?

KOKUMA: We go to Bostin still yes?

JULIA ELIZABETH: I didn't know what to do anymore. Can't go home. Can't stay here after seeing what we just did. No…

KOKUMA: Mistress? We still go to Bostin yes?

JULIA ELIZABETH: No child… No child, they'll be looking for us there… We must journey on… We must journey farther.

KOKUMA: There are lands farther than Bostin?

JULIA ELIZABETH: Yes dear, there's land farther than Boston.
Come follow me.
Well climb this hill, I'll show you.

MAWU: Julia took Kokuma's hand as they trudged up the hill, climbed it to it's very top and sat upon the rock. High above the fog, they could survey the land ahead of them. Kokuma sat upon a rock. Julia pointed to the grand expanse of land that was this strange place called America.

(JULIA ELIZABETH *points eastward.*)

JULIA ELIZABETH: Look over there just a few more miles that way and we'd be on the outskirts of Boston.

KOKUMA: And we no go there?

JULIA ELIZABETH: No…no won't be safe. We'll go that way.
(She changes the direction she points.)

KOKUMA: What is that way?

JULIA ELIZABETH: Mr Librance had acquired land in the Ohio River area. He was planning to sell before fate struck, due to it being Abolishionist land… You'd be in freedman country we get across that river.

KOKUMA: Freedman?

JULIA ELIZABETH: It means you won't be bound by anyone. You'll be a free woman.

(KOKUMA *closes her eyes and takes a deep breath.*)

KOKUMA: Free.
I like this word Free.

(JULIA ELIZABETH *sits down next to* KOKUMA.)

JULIA ELIZABETH: Free
Yes, I must admit I, I too like that word
(She closes her eyes, and takes a deep breath.)
Come on child, let's go.

KOKUMA: No. No wait… Can we…Can we sit here a while longer?

JULIA ELIZABETH: The Librance Brothers they could be—

KOKUMA: Please… Just a little for a while little long.

JULIA ELIZABETH: Why?

KOKUMA: Cause for the first time here I can see where freedom is.
Beautiful.

JULIA ELIZABETH: Beautiful.
(She takes a deep breath and coughs. Coughs hard. She wipes her mouth upon her sleeve. There's blood. Lots of it. She coughs some more.)

KOKUMA: Finally we move forward. We move down the hill slowly weaving our way down the rocky path and entered the woods, the woods held shadows and in them under the thick canopy of trees there would be found safety.

JULIA ELIZABETH: I think we can rest here child.

KOKUMA: Is it safe to start a fire?

JULIA ELIZABETH: I think so… But just a small one.

KOKUMA: And start one we did.

JULIA ELIZABETH: Is it true? What you said couple of days ago, about my husband… about him…raping you while I was downstairs entertaining? Is it true?

KOKUMA: A woman knows who their husband is.

(Silence)

JULIA ELIZABETH: I'm sorry.
If… If…I had known…
If I had…
I thought you would be too young for him.
I thought I was doing the right thing.
I thought if I named you after our lost daughter, if I kept you under my care, it would…
I don't know what to say…
I had just hoped—

KOKUMA: I carry his child.

(*Silence*)

JULIA ELIZABETH: Are you certain?

KOKUMA: Yes mistress.

JULIA ELIZABETH: Don't…Don't call me that… no need
to call me that ever again.
Julia… You can call me Julia, Julia Elizabeth. I own you
no longer. We're almost to Ohio, you'll be free there.
We'll both be free there.
Ah my hand are trembling. God look at me. Words
failing me now. Here I am not sure to be mad at
myself, him, or you. I feel like… Like I've betrayed
you child. I feel like I failed myself. I'm just as guilty…
I'm…I'm sorry… Maybe you're right child. Maybe my
people are the savages.

WEST: Kokuma and Julia sit there the soft glow of the
campfire warming them in silence.

KOKUMA: And then when the quiet could be taken no
longer.
Mistress…I mean Julia reaches into her bag pulls out a
small leather bound book.
You read now?

JULIA ELIZABETH: Yes my love. I'm going to read now.

KOKUMA: Will you read to me?
Like you use to do?

(*Silence*)

JULIA ELIZABETH: I'll do even better…I'll teach you how
to read it.

KOKUMA: You'll teach me? Why would you do this?

JULIA ELIZABETH: Because…because I see something
special about you.
This book is what's called the bible.

One of the few books I brought with me from Boston,
Reminds me of home.

WEST: And teach her she did that night as the soft glow
from the campfire illuminated the pages,

SOUTH: And when they had finished the lesson for the
night.

WEST: Kokuma pulled out from her small bag a hair
brush.

SOUTH: The same hair brush that had been used
time after time on Mr. Librance estate, to brush Julia
Elizabeth's hair.

JULIA ELIZABETH: My brush. I thought I had lost it.

KOKUMA: May I brush your hair?

JULIA ELIZABETH: That would be nice… but no…this
time…this time let me brush yours.

WEST: Julia brushing the girls hair, Kokuma slowly
learning how to read the markings in the book.

(End scene)

BOOK FOUR
PILGRIMAGE IN THE MOONLIGHT

*(*MAWU *appears bangs her staff three times.* JULIA
ELIZABETH *and* KOKUMA *step out of the darkness.)*

KOKUMA: Still aware of the dangers that lurk behind
us we journey on. Brief stops made to seek out food,
or to teach me my lessons in reading. I forgot how I
had once wished Julia dead. Strange how forgiving of
crimes my people are to those who have done us harm.

KOKUMA: Morning… Into Night.

CHORUS: Night…into Morning.

KOKUMA: Morning… Into Night.

JULIA ELIZABETH: Three more days have passed without encountering the Librance brothers, my hopes that perhaps they went to Boston to catch me at my fathers home started to rise a bit more. We journeyed on.

KOKUMA: The sky above a starless night offered no light to see by except for the moon above. It was larger than I've ever seen and hung low.

JULIA ELIZABETH: We journeyed on…I coughed into my kerchief. Blood soaked. I hid it quickly so the girl wouldn't see.

KOKUMA: I saw.

JULIA ELIZABETH: We journeyed on.

KOKUMA: Up a hill and down another.

JULIA ELIZABETH: We stayed off the main roads.

KOKUMA: Kept close to the comforting shadows of the trees.

JULIA ELIZABETH: We rounded a bend and the girl stopped.

KOKUMA: Do you see?

JULIA ELIZABETH: I saw but couldn't believe.

KOKUMA: A small figure in the distant standing at the crossroads looking upwards towards the moon above.

JULIA ELIZABETH: But that wasn't what caused us to stop in our path.

KOKUMA: Seemed like all the light of the moon seemed to both shine down upon her.

JULIA ELIZABETH: And yet come from her.

KOKUMA: What do we do?

JULIA ELIZABETH: That was a damn good question.

KOKUMA: What do we do?

JULIA ELIZABETH: I hadn't had a single mapped out plan of action this entire journey and yet now this girl desires to ask me for guidance.

I don't know child…I don't know…

We stood there for what seemed like forever before the figure in the light turned their attention upon us. And waved us forward.

(MAWU *waves out toward the audience.*)

KOKUMA: We drew closer to the stranger and as we grew closer…

JULIA ELIZABETH: And closer.

KOKUMA: We saw that it was…

JULIA ELIZABETH: An old white woman. Small and bent over.

KOKUMA: A beautiful woman of chocolate brown skin. Dressed in the garb of my homeland.

JULIA ELIZABETH: Her skin wrinkled from time.

KOKUMA: Her eyes wandered over us.

JULIA ELIZABETH: Eyes almond shaped.

KOKUMA: Eyes black as the night.

JULIA ELIZABETH: Eyes yellow…golden yellow.

KOKUMA: Bare feet

JULIA ELIZABETH: Hair silvered.

KOKUMA: She smiled.

JULIA ELIZABETH: She smiled.

KOKUMA: She smiled.

JULIA ELIZABETH: She smiled, a crescent moon of a smile.

KOKUMA:	JULIA ELIZABETH:
The beautiful woman.	The Old time weary woman.

JULIA ELIZABETH: Smile and nodded at us. Spoke nothing and drew close to us.

KOKUMA: Her breath reminded me of…

JULIA ELIZABETH: Red wine, and—

KOKUMA: The berries and the agbayun of my home, the smell of—

JULIA ELIZABETH: Christmas. Dinners at my fathers home. The aroma of old leather, and his smoking pipe. Turkey and—

KOKUMA: Goat and salted fish cooked over the open fire—

JULIA ELIZABETH: She smelled like my…

KOKUMA:	JULIA ELIZABETH:
My mother…	My mother…

KOKUMA: My mother.

JULIA ELIZABETH: She smelled of the—

KOKUMA / JULIA ELIZABETH: The ocean…

KOKUMA: And if the moonlight and the night had a smell that could be described in words…

CHORUS: She would possess it.

KOKUMA: She moved closer to us,

CHORUS: Glided towards us.

KOKUMA: Her hands gently touched our faces.

(MAWU *touches their faces.*)

(*She picks back up her staff bangs it three times to the earth.*)

KOKUMA: I found myself floating…

JULIA ELIZABETH: Floating…

KOKUMA: Floating in the moonlight.

JULIA ELIZABETH: I must be in some kind of trance…

KOKUMA: This must be the land between sleep and awake.

JULIA ELIZABETH: No fear in my heart… Just—

KOKUMA: I felt washed in tears…

JULIA ELIZABETH: Washed in sadness…that between moment of lost and finding something sacred—

KOKUMA: Desolation, grief, loneliness… all those feels wrapped itself around us.

(The wind around them begins to rises.)

KOKUMA / JULIA ELIZABETH: Then she spoke.

MAWU: Hello my daughters.

KOKUMA: Mawu? Great mother is that you?

JULIA ELIZABETH: Who are you? What are you?

MAWU: A Messenger… A bearer of gifts.

JULIA ELIZABETH: A messenger of what?

KOKUMA: Gifts? What gifts have you given me?

MAWU: Hope.
Change.
The future.
Sorrow…pain…joy…redemption…

KOKUMA: The wind starts to whisper our names.

(The sound of the winds chanting, drums beating. The WINDS *dance.)*

KOKUMA: She touches my stomach and I feel it stretch and grow.
Oh the pain!!!

JULIA ELIZABETH: She touches my chest…I feel a
warmth take over my body… And then I see him… My
husband standing there looking at me.

MAWU: I'm Mother Moon, I not just illuminate the
truth, I reflect it as well my children.

KOKUMA: Oh it hurts!!!!

MAWU: Some times you need to experience the pain
before you can discover joy.

JULIA ELIZABETH: There he stood my husband, reaching
out towards me…pointing at me accusingly.

KOKUMA: Stop the pain!!!!

JULIA ELIZABETH: Looking at me with those empty
eyes… Like I was equally to blame.

MAWU: Think about your journey thus far.

JULIA ELIZABETH: I pressed my hands to my face
trying to tear the image of him but all I saw was pretty
dresses, and carriage rides,
Slave auctions and beating…
Children ripped from mothers' arms.

KOKUMA: It hurts!!! It hurts so much!!!

MAWU: See what you've done.

KOKUMA: Mother Moon!!! Mother Moon stop this
please!!! My stomach it hurts!!!

MAWU: I'm bearing gifts and messages child, it will
only last a while.

JULIA ELIZABETH: All I saw was my husband kicking
me in belly.
Beating me till my child died inside me…
Beat me till I became childless and cold.
My Abigail gone!

KOKUMA: Why are you doing this?!!!! Oooowwww!!!

JULIA ELIZABETH: Me turning away as my husband raping my servant girls, their bellies swelling with child, rage, rage, rage!!!!

MAWU: Do you see what you need to see Julia? Do you understand your purpose Kokuma?

JULIA ELIZABETH: My maids one after another belly swelling. Standing on the balcony.
Push.Push. Push…
So simple. One after another. Librance way.
I was no better than them. I was guilty of the same horrible crimes,
I hated my husband for.

KOKUMA: Help me… help me…

JULIA ELIZABETH: My husbands laughing…

(The NORTH WIND *turns into Librance. He laughs. It echoes through* JULIA ELIZABETH.*)*

*(*JULIA ELIZABETH *coughs up more blood. Vomits it)*

*(*KOKUMA *drops to her knees her belly swelling with life.)*

(Blackness)

(The sound of a baby crying)

KOKUMA: And then she's gone. Us alone at the crossroads. A small infant child in my arms, Julia Elizabeth curled in a ball, drenched in her own blood and sweat. Only the sound of her voice can be heard inside of my head.

(As KOKUMA speaks, she is joined by the voice of MAWU. They speak the first sentence together in unison and then MAWU's voice takes over.

KOKUMA / MAWU: Can you hear me, my child…listen well.

MAWU: From you… From this child you hold. Birthed from sorrow and rage. Generations shall flow from you… the children from your line will be prophets and preachers, storytellers and teachers. They'll survive hangmen nooses, and barking dogs, bombed churches and burning crosses. But above all else…the children that come from your line will lead our people in the times to come… They will be forever the blessed ones. Don't be afraid, I will never leave you.

KOKUMA: And then the voice was gone again. Me with a child. Barely a child myself and Julia… Poor Julia Elizabeth. Shivering…scared…stared looking about filled with fear and uncertainty. Shaking her head from side to side. Blood stained her dress. Her once beautiful beautiful hair now silver like the moon. The meeting with the mother moon had changed her. We sat at the crossroads. Till the moon faded into the sunlight. Till night turned to morning.

JULIA ELIZABETH: She spoke to me.

KOKUMA: She did?
What did she tell you?

JULIA ELIZABETH: It'll be alright…
We'll be alright…
We'll be alright…

(End scene)

BOOK FIVE
THE CRUEL PRICE OF FREEDOM

(KOKUMA sings. JULIA ELIZABETH and MAWU stand behind them.)

KOKUMA:
Ti wa ni free ni ofe baba… Mo ti yio padanu ti o bẹ.
(Be free, be free father, I shall miss you so.)
Ni ofe, ni ofe iya … Mo ti yio padanu ti o bẹ.
(Be free, be free mother, I shall miss you so.)

Wo lori mi bi mo ti sun…
(Watch over me as I sleep)
Wo lori mi bi mo ti sun…
(Watch over me as I sleep)

(A blanket of fog covers the stage.)

MaAWU: They stand there unmoved upon the crossroads before they continued on. Traveled through foothills and and meadows, slept where they could at nights, ate when they could. With a renewed energy coursing through her… Julia Elizabeth lead the way as Kokuma held her child as they journeyed forward. As they drew closer to the Ohio. Their lungs began to fill with liberty.

JULIA ELIZABETH: Have you thought of a name for him yet?

KOKUMA: I don't know yet. This baby, he's a stranger to me. All I can do is love it though.

JULIA ELIZABETH: You should give it a name.

KOKUMA: Perhaps I will name him… Chinua, after my father.

JULIA ELIZABETH: You can't give that baby a name like that.

KOKUMA: Why not? It is a good name. It is my father's name.

JULIA ELIZABETH: He'd never survive in America with that kind of a name.
You need to give him a good Christian sorts of a name.

KOKUMA: Perhaps. What would you name a boy?

JULIA ELIZABETH: Me?

KOKUMA: Yes you.

JULIA ELIZABETH: I've never been the sorts to name boys, always imagined me with a girls… Sadly I'll

never know children no longer. But…I suppose if I was
to name me a boy, I'd name him Christopher.

KOKUMA: I like this name…Christopher. I shall name
him Christopher. But in the quiet hours…when I am
alone with him, he shall be Chinua.

JULIA ELIZABETH: I marveled at how much Kokuma,
my Abigail, had matured since the crossroad. More
sure of herself she was. No longer a child but a woman
she was becoming. I could see it in her walk, in those
eyes. We had traveled so far…so far…from southward
to north. Thousands of miles we journeyed. The sky
above us changed from a precious blue to grey to cruel
dark. As the clouds began to grumble.

KOKUMA: Storm coming.

JULIA ELIZABETH: Yes, this I know… this I know.

KOKUMA: We went on. Pushed on. Til the rain started
to fall. Luck would have it we found an old abandoned
shack. Water dripped through the boards that served
as a roof above us. Forming small puddles on the floor.

JULIA ELIZABETH: Kokuma slept. Me holding the child
in my arms.
We looked at each other.
Something about those child's eyes.
I found solace in that child's eyes.
Seemed to look into the depth of my soul.
Thunder and lightning filled the night and that child
refused to cry.
Just looking at me.
Staring into my eyes. It was in that child's eyes a vision
came… or something of that nature.
The trees sharpen,
A shadowy figure of a tiny girl walking cradling a
child.

The world black and white and lonely greys as if it
were a carpet of snow and black crows flying about.
A buzzing in my ears, something like a distant music.
Words to a song I've never heard before.
No image of me in sight…
This was a peculiar child. Finally I fell asleep, cradling
that infant in my arms as his dear mother slept… The
sound of the rain pounding against the wood. When I
woke up again…

(Sound of a revolver clicking.)

JULIA ELIZABETH: Staring down at me with a gun
pointed at me was Junior Librance. We had been
careless.

NORTH: *(As JUNIOR)* Good morning, Miss Librance, my
brother and myself have been looking for ya, seems
you took both a sibling relations from me and it would
seem a great deal of money.

JULIA ELIZABETH: We spent the money. There ain't no
money left.

NORTH: *(As JUNIOR)* You spent the money, Oh words
that should never uttered from your mouth. Especially
when you got this young gal and her niglet in your
care. No no no…those words aren't acceptable dear.

JULIA ELIZABETH: I swear it. All I hold is the papers for
land held in Ohio. That's all.

NORTH: *(As JUNIOR)* We'll that's not what I need to be
hearing.

JULIA ELIZABETH: I look to my left and there the child
held by the throat, standing upon her tippy toes.
Struggling to breathe. Pearson's grip tightening.
Let her go…let her go. You got me. Just let the child
and her baby be free.

NORTH: (*As* JUNIOR) Golly, look at you Julia, these roads seemed to have aged you. You got me curious though why you so concerned about this little nigra? What oh, what could it be? Let's find out now…

JULIA ELIZABETH: He snatches the infant away. Puts the gun to its head.

KOKUMA: Not my baby!

NORTH: (*As* JUNIOR) Ever skin an animal? Dipped your hands in its life blood. Nothing like it. You know there is an art to skinning an animal alive.

JULIA ELIZABETH: Please don't. We don't have the money…we don't have any money.

NORTH: (*As* JUNIOR) First you start around the throat… Carve right around it. Till there is a nice open…then you slice the belly from the dick on up til you reach the throat.

KOKUMA: Don't hurt my baby.

NORTH: (*As* JUNIOR) Then all you got to do is peel back that skin. That's the easy part…I've never done it on a niglet baby before but I'm quite certain that it is similar to carving up a rabbit. Who knows…maybe I'll make a little hat out of him.

JULIA ELIZABETH: There's no money. Let the baby go.

KOKUMA: I have the money!

(*Silence*)

NORTH: (*As* JUNIOR) What was that?

KOKUMA: I have the money. The money that you want I have it.

NORTH: (*As* JUNIOR) Well look at that, one of you actually has a lick of common sense to her. Funny I never thought it would be the girl. Pearson let her go. Get me my money, girl.

KOKUMA: Give me my baby. Give me my boy.

NORTH: *(As* JUNIOR*)* Oh no…get me my money, in fact why don't you go on and put it down right here. Put it down! So if you get so inclined to pull something well I'll just kick that baby's head clean off. Now get me that damn money!!!

JULIA ELIZABETH: What are you doing child?

KOKUMA: I must protect my baby. I must do what is asked of me.

JULIA ELIZABETH: Pearson released her and she guided him to one of the sacks.
She reaches down. Opens it.
Pulls out the scissors.
The same scissors used night after night to trim my hair.
The same scissors that killed my husband.
She turned, jumped upward and jabbed it in his neck.
Pearson dropped to the floor.
Blood. So much blood.
Junior screamed…turned his gun towards Abigail.
He stood over her child.
My Abigail.
She may not have been birthed from me but she was my daughter…and a mother's rage.
A mother's rage is one that no man wants to cross.

KOKUMA: Julia flew towards the man.

WEST: She grabbed at him.
Hands reaching for anything to grab.

KOKUMA: Ripping at his eyes,

EAST: Clothes

KOKUMA: Face…

WEST: Wrestling for the gun.

EAST: The infant screaming in terror.

KOKUMA: They crashed backwards.
And a gun shot rang out.
Followed by another.

(Darkness)

KOKUMA: We unlatched the door stepped outside that shack.
There stood six gun men, standing there guns pointed at us.
No hope in sight, I did the only thing I could.
I opened the pouch…
Thousands of midnight black crows flew out.
Darkness covered the world… And we walked forward.
We walked past them unseen like—

(MAWU raises her staff high.)

KOKUMA / JULIA ELIZABETH: Like we were ghosts.

JULIA ELIZABETH: We went on stumbling away from them.
Kokuma held the baby close to her.

KOKUMA: We walked till we couldn't walk any longer.

JULIA ELIZABETH: Walked til our legs gave out on us.

KOKUMA: Julia bent over holding her side before she finally collapsed and laid there shivering.

JULIA ELIZABETH: Cough

KOKUMA: Cough

JULIA ELIZABETH: The taste of blood in my mouth.

KOKUMA: I pull her close.
Wetness…warm slick wetness. I pull my hands away.
Blood.
She was bleeding from her side.

Coughing up blood, blood pouring from the wound in her side.
I sat beside her cradling Julia in one arm, my child in the other.

JULIA ELIZABETH: I can't…I can't go any farther.

KOKUMA: We're not far. Get up. We can make it.

JULIA ELIZABETH: This is as far I go I'm afraid….
I want you to have something.
(She pulls out of from her apron a paper.)

KOKUMA: What's this?

JULIA ELIZABETH: It's the deed.
It's the deed to your new home in Ohio.
It's not much but it'll be home for you.
For you and that baby.

KOKUMA: I'm scared.

JULIA ELIZABETH: I know, but you'll manage to be alright.
You're free.
You're a free woman. You're son will grow up free.
Take the paper, child.

*(*KOKUMA *takes it.)*

KOKUMA: Come on we must go.

JULIA ELIZABETH: I can't. I want to…I want to rest here.
Kokuma?

KOKUMA: Yes?

JULIA ELIZABETH: Whatever you do, child, whatever you do…survive.

KOKUMA: Yes ma'am…

JULIA ELIZABETH: Kokuma?

KOKUMA: Yes?

JULIA ELIZABETH: Look over there… You see that? Are you looking?

KOKUMA: I'm looking.

JULIA ELIZABETH: I can see where freedom is. Beautiful.

KOKUMA: Beautiful.
And with that she coughed one last time.
Took a deep breath and died in my arms.
Her eyes looking at the sun setting in the distance.
I kissed her on the forehead.
Rose to my feet, child in arm.
Took all that I needed from her in one bag.
A pendant with a crescent moon, her brush, a few scraps of food… And…the deed.
I walk on.
Journeyed onward towards freedom.
Crows gathered around me. Seemed to lead me forward.
Part of me said I should stay to the woods, but a quiet voice guided me down the road.
Whispering to me with every step.
Walked by farmhouse after farmhouse.
An elderly black woman approached me. Basket in one hand humming a song to herself as walked towards me.
Humming to herself a song strange yet familiar.
Do you I stay…do I run…

MAWU: Hello child.
(*Silence*)
You look like you and that baby been travelling quite aways.

KOKUMA: Yes ma'am.

MAWU: You eat. Seems to me you could use yourself a meal and nice bed for the night.
People around these parts call me Old Lady Goody. What's yours?

KOKUMA: My name?

MAWU: You got a name now dontcha?

(Silence. Long silence)

MAWU: Well child, you gonna answer?

KOKUMA: My name...my name is... My mother birthed me Kokumathey named me Abigail...but I call myself... Julia.

MAWU: Well child, it's nice to meet ya,
I got some beans and rice on the pot, and nice bed for your baby and you.
Come on child, let's go home.
Looks like you're getting blessed today.

KOKUMA: Yes...yes I am.

(As MAWU *guides* KOKUMA *away. She sings.)*

CHORUS: *(Sings as they enter overlapping* MAWU's *words)*
Ose ayo,
A-beh A-deh o,
Ah-eh-o *(X3)*

END OF PLAY

www.ingramcontent.com/pod-product-compliance
Lightning Source LLC
Chambersburg PA
CBHW070023110426
42741CB00034B/2386